D1566235

FERGUSON
CAREER BIOGRAPHIES

THEODOR SEUSS
GEISEL

Author and Illustrator

Todd Peterson

Ferguson
An imprint of Infobase Publishing

Theodor Seuss Geisel: Author and Illustrator

Copyright © 2006 by Infobase Publishing

Ferguson
An imprint of Infobase Publishing
132 West 31st Street
New York NY 10001

Library of Congress Cataloging-in-Publication Data

Peterson, Todd (Todd D.), 1969–
   Theodor Seuss Geisel : author and illustrator / Todd Peterson.
      p. cm.
   Includes index.
   ISBN 0-8160-6105-X (alk. paper)
  1. Seuss, Dr. 2. Authors, American—20th century—Biography. 3. Illustrators—United States—Biography. 4. Illustration of books—United States. 5. Children's literature—Authorship. I. Title.
  PS3513.E2Z795 2006
  813'.52—dc22   2005033786

Ferguson books are available at special discounts when purchased in bulk quantities for businesses, associations, institutions, or sales promotions. Please call our Special Sales Department in New York at (212) 967-8800 or (800) 322-8755.

You can find Ferguson on the World Wide Web at http://www.fergpubco.com

Text design by David Strelecky

Pages 87–113 adapted from Ferguson's *Encyclopedia of Careers and Vocational Guidance, Thirteenth Edition.*

Printed in the United States of America

MP FOF 10 9 8 7 6 5 4 3 2 1

This book is printed on acid-free paper.

CONTENTS

1

THE CAT IN THE HAT

Two hundred twenty-three words—that was all it took to change the world of children's books for good. They were 223 short words too, selected from a list that had been approved for readers of all ages. "Cat" and "hat," the first two words on the list that rhymed with one another, became the basis for the story, and the rest of the book followed from that title: *The Cat in the Hat*. When Theodor Geisel—known around the world as Dr. Seuss—finished that book in 1957, the renowned children's author was halfway through what had already been a successful career. Ted, as he was known, had once planned on becoming an English professor. Instead he had grown into a well-known artist with a lucrative career sketching advertisements. He had also become a respected children's book author and, briefly, enjoyed success as an award-winning filmmaker. But when *The Cat in the Hat* appeared, Dr.

Seuss's work grew in popularity. It was immediately apparent with *Cat* that he and his publishers had a hit on their hands. The title was soon flying off shelves, and bookstores doubled their initial orders for copies of Dr. Seuss's new children's book. Within three years, nearly a million copies of *The Cat in the Hat* would find their way into readers' hands, as the book was translated into several languages, including French, Chinese, and Swedish.

By now these words have become familiar to readers around the world, but despite the book's early success, it would have been impossible then to predict the impact that *The Cat in the Hat*—and Dr. Seuss himself—would have on children's literature. In the more than 47 years since Seuss pieced together those 223 words, the popularity of this author and artist has grown with each passing season. His reputation has not diminished since his death in 1991, and in 2004 readers of all ages around the world celebrated the 100th anniversary of Ted's birth.

The Cat in the Hat changed the way in which people viewed children's books. Until that time, books for very young readers were simple, straightforward, and, according to some critics at that time, boring. *Cat* was also short and simple, but despite its length and uncomplicated story line about a rebellious cat who, with the help of Thing One and Thing Two, turns the home of two young children into a complete mess, it was not so simple to write.

Through his drawings and writing, Theodor Seuss Geisel (seen here reading to a group of children) changed the way people viewed children's books. (Getty Images)

A Difficult Cat

When Theodor Geisel (pronounced *Guy*-zel) accepted the assignment from his publisher to write a children's book that would excite young readers in the way that typical grade-school primers had failed to do, he had already been writing for children for 20 years. Some of Ted's titles had already become best-sellers, including his first children's title, *And to Think That I Saw It on Mulberry Street,* as well as *Horton Hatches the Egg, If I Ran the Zoo,* and *Horton Hears a Who!,* among others. But his true love had always been drawing, and he had been trying to find a way to devote all his time to working on his children's titles. The money he had made from the books he had already written did not seem like enough to live on, but just a few years earlier he had abandoned most of his other work to focus exclusively on children's books.

It was at the urging of William Spaulding, a friend who worked at the publishing house Houghton Mifflin, that Ted accepted *The Cat in the Hat* project. Spaulding challenged Ted to write and illustrate "a story that first-graders can't put down." Spaulding handed Ted a list of 225 words that could be used in the story, and the author agreed to take the list home and see what he could come up with.

At the time, Ted had other projects in the works. He was finishing a version of *If I Ran the Circus*, a follow-up to his successful *If I Ran the Zoo*, first published in 1950. Ted put Spaulding's list away on his desk, where it sat for several months while the artist worked on his other projects. When he returned to *The Cat in the Hat*, he thought the book would be easy to write. "I remember thinking that I might be able to dash off *The Cat in the Hat* in two or three weeks," he once said. When he returned to the 225-word list, however, Ted experienced an exercise in frustration.

Ted told at least a couple different stories about the first drafts and origin of his new children's book. In one version, he first imagined a story that used two of his favorite words, "queen" and "zebra." The title, he said, would be *The Queen Zebra,* and Ted quickly began filling pages when it occurred to him to check the word list. Neither "queen" nor "zebra" appeared on the list of words he could use.

Next he imagined a story about a bird, but the word "bird" was not on the list either. With a little imagination, his bird became a "wing thing"—both words appeared on the list—and as he further searched the list, Dr. Seuss found that he could also use the word "fly." But that was about the only other word that pertained to "wing thing," he later wrote in an essay. After a month and a half, he said, he had to give up. "My 'wing thing' couldn't have 'legs' or a 'beak' or a 'tail.' . . . And she couldn't lay 'eggs,'" he said, running through several words he thought would have been important to the story but that were not on the list. It was, Ted said, like making "apple strudel without the strudels."

In a different version in which he recounted his inspiration for the first draft, Ted said he initially wanted to write a story about scaling Mt. Everest while the temperature was 60 degrees below zero. When he told his publisher about the story, the publisher agreed that it was a fine idea. "However, you can't use the word 'scaling,' you can't use the word 'peaks,' you can't use 'Everest,' you can't use 'sixty' and you can't use 'degrees,'" the publisher told him.

It was not until he produced a drawing of a cat in a hat, and hit on the words "cat" and "hat," that the book began to take shape for him. As he worked, the story began to unfold, but it took him nearly a year to complete the book. "Writing children's books is hard work, a lot harder than most people realize," he said. "You try telling a pretty complicated story using less than 250 words!" The key, he explained, was a willingness to rewrite and rewrite—as many times as was necessary.

"It took a year of getting mad as blazes and throwing the [book] across the room," Ted later said. "You get to a place where for want of a word you can't tell a story." But when he was finished, *The Cat in the Hat* delighted young readers who many adults thought were turning away from books.

An Unwitting Educator

Ted had been writing children's books for nearly 20 years when he began *The Cat in the Hat*, so his audience was not new to him. What was different—and would lead to his being viewed as an educator rather than just a children's author—was the cultural climate in which Ted was enlisted to write *Cat*. In the mid-1950s, many educators and parents were concerned that children were not reading as much as they had in the past. Adults worried that

A scene from the animated version of Dr. Seuss's classic book
The Cat in the Hat. (Photofest)

new temptations, such as television, were causing young people to lose interest in reading.

One book in particular, *Why Johnny Can't Read,* by Rudolf Flesch, would have a lasting effect in its criticism of teachers' methods. Not only did the author criticize the way in which children were being taught but also the books they were given to read. These stories, often referred to as "Dick and Jane" books, were labeled "dull" and "simplistic." It was in a *Life* magazine article in 1954 that the novelist John Hersey first suggested Dr. Seuss as a potential author of instructional schoolbooks for young readers.

Hersey had named Seuss as an author who could potentially "make reading fun" for children, a suggestion that Ted wholeheartedly endorsed—until he began writing *The Cat in the Hat*. "All I needed . . . was to find a whale of an exciting subject which would make the average six-year-old want to read like crazy," Ted said at the time. "None of the old dull stuff: Dick has a ball. Dick likes the ball. The ball is red, red, red, red."

Ted understood the value of repetition, but he knew that simply repeating a word over and over without the benefit of a good story around it was not going to hold the interest of young readers. Instead, his repetitions were worked into verses, where key words would naturally occur repeatedly within the story. There were other elements that he felt were necessary to a good book, among them humor. "[Kids] want to laugh at something that's ridiculous," he said.

It was out of that way of thinking that the crazy cat that unexpectedly drops in on a couple of children was born. The Cat is a departure from Ted's previous animals such as Horton, the long-suffering elephant, or Thidwick, the patient moose. The Cat is mischievous and, with the assistance of Thing One and Thing Two, destructive. The two otherwise well-behaved children find themselves in a house turned upside down that must be put back together before their mother returns. While the Cat does help the children put everything back in its proper place, his juggling antics are nothing like the animals Ted had created before. With *The Cat in the Hat*, Ted's animals were now the types of creatures that would capture a first-grader's attention—and hold it.

A New Beginning in Children's Literature

Children were not the only readers impressed with Dr. Seuss's new Cat. John Hersey, whose *Life* magazine essay had initially inspired Ted, called the book "[a] gift to the art of reading." A writer for the *Saturday Review* said Dr. Seuss had written a story "which presents an impelling incentive to read."

The reaction at Random House, the publisher that put out the trade edition (the edition sold in bookstores; Houghton Mifflin released the school edition of the book) was to launch Beginner Books, a line of titles aimed at young readers of which Ted would be president. Random House would distribute the titles, while Ted and his wife, Helen, would operate the imprint, with the help of Phyllis Cerf, wife of Random House head Bennett Cerf. These titles for young readers would be separate from the rest of Dr. Seuss's books (which Ted called his "big books"), and he and Helen would exercise a great deal of control over the other authors hired to contribute to the Beginner series.

Despite the fact that these were short books, many authors found it difficult to come up with a compelling story given the few words they had at their disposal. Most of them discovered that building an interesting story out of fewer than 300 words was nearly impossible. Ted, however, was just discovering just how much he could say in very few words. By the end of the year, he had received nearly five tons of fan mail, and he had been asked to speak and appear at countless events—an especially difficult task, since he suffered extreme stage fright. In 1958 *The Cat in the Hat* was selling 500 copies a day, and the name "Dr. Seuss" would soon be permanently linked to children's literature.

2

ART FROM THE START

Theodor Seuss Geisel was born in Springfield, Massachusetts, on March 2, 1904. The son of Theodor Robert and Henrietta Geisel (whose maiden name was Seuss), young Ted came into the world in a house just around the corner from Henrietta's father's bakery. The Seuss family, whose name was originally pronounced *zoice*, were German immigrants, as was the Geisel family. Ted was the second child, following an older sister named Margarthea, who insisted that her name was "Marnie Mecca Ding Ding Guy." People eventually began calling her Marnie. A third child, Henrietta, was born when Ted was two, but she died from pneumonia when she was 18 months old.

The Geisels operated a brewery called Kalmbach and Geisel, which was started by Ted's grandfather in 1876. Springfield, located just 100 miles west of Boston, was an idyllic place for a young boy. When Ted was two, the family moved to a house on Fairfield Street, where the budding artist would spend the rest of his childhood—and part of his early adult years as well.

The Young Artist

From an early age, Ted had an ear for meter in both English and German, the language spoken at home, and an early knack for rhyming. He also had an impressionable personality, and the people and places of his childhood served as inspiration for his later work.

Springfield's main thoroughfare was Mulberry Street, and from a very young age Ted was fascinated by its bustling activity. Ted would stop and stare as the carriages, cars, and bicycles made their way around one another, frustrating his sister as she tried to drag him to school. These memories would later make their way into his first book, *And to Think That I Saw It on Mulberry Street*. Ted's neighbors left an equally strong impression on him. Real families such as the Wickershams, Terwilligers, and McElligots were never forgotten and later turned up as characters in his books.

Ted was interested in comics and books from the start. His mother, Henrietta, found that she could get Ted to obey her with offers of books in exchange for good behavior. He was equally interested in drawing and art, although Marnie later admitted that she could not always tell what Ted's creatures were supposed to resemble. But his work impressed some people: When he was 12, Ted won first prize for a cartoon of a man reeling in a giant fish that he submitted to the *Springfield Union* newspaper.

Ted's fascination with animals was evident from an early age, and some people have attributed it to a position that his father held later in life. In 1931, long after Ted was an adult, his father was appointed the park superintendent of the local zoo, a position he held for 30 years. When Ted was a boy, however, his father was appointed to the Springfield park board, of which the new zoo was a part. Ted spent many days exploring the park and zoo, with his drawing pad in hand. He trailed his father from cage to cage, sketching animals whose features never quite looked like the animals did in real life. But while Ted was growing up, his father was preparing to take over the family brewery from Ted's grandfather.

The War Effort

In 1917, when Ted was barely a teenager, the United States entered World War I against the central European nations, including Germany. It was a difficult time for German-American immigrants such as Ted's family. People questioned the loyalty of immigrants who had ties to

Germany, and Ted recalled being harassed by other children on more than one occasion.

But the Geisel family's American roots were strong, and Ted, as a Boy Scout, joined the war effort by selling government bonds, the proceeds of which were used to support the troops. When Ted's grandfather heard about the sales drive, he purchased a stack of bonds from his grandson, earning young Ted the rank of second-best sales for the bonds. Just a few months later, however, an event would unfold that would leave Ted scarred for life, when 10 Scouts with the most sales were set to receive awards for their work.

Much of Springfield had turned out to see those Boy Scouts gathered on the stage. Former United States president Theodore Roosevelt was handing out the awards, and Ted was last in line as Roosevelt worked his way down the boys, presenting each with his medal. But when Roosevelt reached Ted, the former president discovered that he had run out of medals. While Ted stood there with his entire family and many people from the town watching, Roosevelt boomed in his deep voice, "What's this little boy doing here?"

Ted was mortified, and the scoutmaster came and quickly herded him off the stage. The scoutmaster's error in providing Roosevelt with too few medals left a lasting and painful impression on young Ted. Never again would he be comfortable in public, and through most of his life the artist would do what he could to avoid appearing in front of large crowds and later on television.

Ted Versus Art

By the end of 1918 World War I had come to an end, and Ted had entered high school. Although his father had hoped Ted would be more of an athlete—Theodor Sr. was an expert marksman and tried to interest Ted in various sports—the younger Geisel spent most of his time pursuing artistic endeavors. Ted was drawing cartoons and writing short comedic verses for the student newspaper, the *Central Recorder*, which he later edited. He also submitted some of his work under a pseudonym that he would employ later in his career: T.S. LeSieg (Geisel spelled backward).

It was while he was in high school that Ted would have another encounter that would distinctly shape his future. Ted had enrolled in an art class, where students were asked to work on a still-life drawing of flowers that had been placed in a milk-bottle vase. As Ted worked on his sketch, he turned his pad upside-down to draw the flowers from a different angle. His teacher, when she noticed that he was working that way, reprimanded him: "No, Theodor," she said. "Not upside down! There are rules that every artist must abide by. You will never succeed if you break them." Despite his love of drawing, Ted quickly

Ted started taking art classes in high school and soon realized his passion and talent for drawing. (Time Life Pictures/Getty Images)

transferred out of the class, happy to be "free forever from art-by-the-rule books."

Ted would later recall this incident many times as one of the reasons why he never learned to draw—at least not formally. But the young artist was already well on his way to developing his own unique talent, whether it corresponded with the "correct" way to do things or not. His fellow students recognized his abilities, and as Ted finished high school he was voted Class Artist and Class Wit.

On to Dartmouth

Big changes were on the horizon for the Geisel family. In 1919 the federal government ratified Prohibition, the 18th Amendment to the U.S. Constitution, which banned the sale, transportation, or manufacturing of alcoholic beverages in the United States. The ruling was a tremendous blow to the Geisels, whose business was making and selling beer. Ted's father had recently taken over the family business from Ted's grandfather, but when Prohibition became law, the business all but came to an end.

Ted, meanwhile, had to consider his future. He was not sure exactly what he wanted to do, but on the advice of one of his high school teachers Ted applied to Dartmouth College in New Hampshire. He had not been the best student in high school, but Ted had earned decent grades and the Ivy League school was in the process of diversifying its student body. Ted received a good recommendation from an alumnus of the school, and in 1921 he entered Dartmouth with plans to study English.

Even though he didn't fit the typical mold of a scholar, Ted liked his school experience from the start. Almost from the first day he was drawn to the campus humor magazine, *Jack-O-Lantern*, known among the student body as *Jacko*. He started spending a good deal of time at the magazine's editorial offices, and early on he submitted one of his first illustrations to the publication. Ted's persistence impressed some of the upperclassmen, and he quickly made a name for himself at the magazine.

Despite the urging of his parents, Ted was not a remarkable student. He devoted his time to the magazine, and his grades hovered barely above a C average. But Ted's dedication to his craft quickly became apparent: He enrolled in an advertising class where he learned the importance of the color red in capturing a viewer's attention. In botany and zoology classes Ted spent more time sketching plants and animals than he spent studying. One such drawing of a professor's dog—to which Ted added antlers—was an early indication of where his work was headed.

Ted's involvement with *Jacko* grew, and he told one of his close friends that he intended to become the editor of the magazine as soon as he was able. By his sophomore year, Ted's cartoons were a regular feature in the publication. Ted also played the mandolin in the orchestra and wrote occasional news items for the regular college newspaper. He also managed the soccer team and argued for the debate team as well.

A Seuss Emerges

If Ted's upbringing in Springfield had influenced the artist, several other characteristics of the man who would come to be known as Dr. Seuss began to emerge at Dartmouth, too. It was while he was in school that Ted first began wearing a bowtie, which would become one of his trademarks as his stature grew. And Ted was still busy collecting thoughts, ideas, and people for his future stories. It was one of Ted's professors who first uttered the line, "Oh, the places you'll go," which stuck with Ted through his life and eventually became the title of one of his final books.

By the time he was a junior, Ted had become well known around campus. His grades began to improve, and he also started to understand the power of mixing words with his illustrations: "I began to get it through my skull that words and pictures were Yin and Yang . . . that married, might possibly produce a progeny more interesting than either parent," he later said. But it would take Ted nearly 25 years to perfect their union. "At Dartmouth I couldn't even get them engaged," he said.

And as always, Ted's wit and charming personality won him many friends and admirers. A fellow classmate remembered Ted's charisma: "[T]here was no sense of self-importance about him. But when he walked into a room it was like a magician's act. Birds flew out of his hands, and endless bright scarves and fireworks. Everything became brighter, happier, funnier. And he didn't try. Everything Ted did seemed to be a surprise, even to him."

Then, near the end of his junior year in 1924, Ted was elected editor in chief of *Jack-O-Lantern*. He naturally threw himself into his work, spending long hours at the magazine, sometimes toiling through the night. But his work with *Jacko* came to an abrupt halt near the end of his senior year. Ted and some of his friends were caught sharing a small amount of alcohol at a party. With Prohibition being the law of the land, school officials were forced to hand out stiff punishments. Ted was removed from his post as editor in chief of the magazine. But he continued to draw cartoons for the remaining couple issues of *Jacko*, signing his drawings with various pseudonyms, including one under his middle name, Seuss. That would mark the first official appearance of the Seuss name in Ted's work.

As graduation approached, Ted was not sure what he planned to do after college. He had applied for a fellowship study at Oxford University in England, but the student who held the previous year's scholarship was permitted to continue his studies, thereby preventing Ted's potential study. However, Ted had already told his father that he would be attending Oxford on a fellowship—impressive news that the elder Geisel had passed on to the editor of the Springfield newspaper, who had promptly published it in the paper the next day.

Despite Ted's popularity among his friends and fellow students, many of them had questioned his work ethic. Ted was voted "least likely to succeed" by his peers. He lacked focus, and his desire to go to Oxford seemed more borne out of postponing a decision about what to do with his life than a desire to actually continue his English studies.

However, when Ted graduated on June 13, 1925, he had to tell his father that he had not received the Oxford scholarship. But since the news about Ted's acceptance to the prestigious school's scholarship program had already been published, his father agreed that it was necessary to get Ted across the Atlantic and into Oxford, despite the cost. Theodor R. Geisel put up the money for Ted to pursue his studies at Oxford. In late August, Ted sailed for England.

Life and Courtship across the Ocean

At Oxford, Ted enrolled in Lincoln College, one of the university's schools within the school. His plan was to become an English professor, but Ted's experience at his new school was not anything like his years at Dartmouth. For one thing, there was no *Jacko* to which Ted could direct his attention, and from the beginning he never quite felt at home with the rituals and traditions of the school. But while he was there, Ted's dislike of phoniness and his appreciation of the absurd grew.

He spent much of his time in class sketching in the margins of his notebook. In one of his English classes he met Helen Marion Palmer, an American student from New York who was five and a half years older than he was. She noticed his drawings and expressed her admiration for his artistic talent. Helen asked Ted why he was studying to be an English professor when he clearly wanted to draw instead. It did not take Ted long to realize that Helen was right. He knew that he was neither cut out for studying at Oxford nor prepared to become an English professor.

Ted and Helen's relationship grew as his first year at Oxford came to an end. Ted knew he would not be returning to Oxford, but Helen was determined to finish her studies. Yet their future was cemented during a motorcycle outing when Ted, who had taken a turn too fast, skidded into a ditch and sent the couple crashing. The mishap was, Ted later said, cause for the pair to become engaged. By Christmas Helen had returned to the United States for a teaching position. By mid-February 1927 Ted had given up on Europe and sailed for New York.

3

ADS, CARTOONS, AND CHILDREN'S BOOKS

When Ted arrived in New York City he had not completed his Oxford degree, he had no job, and he did not have any prospects on the horizon. The artist was not quite sure what he was going to do with his life, but there was one thing he knew he could count on: Helen. She met Ted when he arrived, and she saw him off as he boarded a train back to Springfield. Ted planned to return to his childhood home while he decided what to do next.

Once there, he set up his drawing board and typewriter and began working up cartoons and stories that he then sent out to editors in New York to see whether or not anyone was interested in his work. But the drawings and humorous items that had amused the readers of *Jack-O-Lantern* did not much impress the editors at first. They really did not know what to make of his work. For one thing, Ted's humor had always been a little bit off the wall. Also, the animals Ted drew did not really look like any animals the editors recognized. But all of that would eventually change.

Logical Insanity

Helen had been Ted's most vocal supporter since she had first seen the animals he was doodling during an English lecture at Oxford. But even she had to concede that Ted's animals were not like any other creatures out there. "Ted's animals are the sort you'd like to take home and meet the family," Helen said. "They have their own world and their own problems and they seem very logical to me."

"Logical insanity" was actually how Ted would later describe his work, particularly as his creatures evolved. If, for example, a creature Ted drew had two heads, logical insanity dictated that it would have to have two toothbrushes as well. But while Ted worked on the particulars of his creatures' existence, he never quite mastered the strict anatomy lessons some artists required. The angles of an animal's body were especially difficult for Ted to

Ted described the creatures he created as products of "logical insanity." (Time Life Pictures/Getty Images)

draw. "Ted never studied the art of anatomy," said Helen. "He puts in joints where he thinks they should be. Elbows and knees have always especially bothered him."

Still, Ted persevered and continued to send out his work. In the spring of 1927 he took a trip to New York, where he went from publishing house to publishing house, trying to interest various editors in his drawings. But the trip did not produce any results. The publishing world was not yet ready for Ted. However, he did not let his lack of success dent his spirit. When he was younger, Ted would often become depressed and morose if things did not go his way. But as he matured Ted was more able to cope with those feelings. So he continued to work on his drawings.

Back in Springfield, he continued sending out his cartoons until finally that summer, a magazine called *The Saturday Evening Post* responded to say that it had purchased one of Ted's cartoons that he had signed "Seuss." Even better, the magazine had included a $25 check as payment for Ted's work. With that, Ted was certain that he had launched a long and successful career with the magazine. He rushed off to tell his parents the good news, then quickly packed his bags, took the remaining money he had managed to save, and headed for New York.

Ted moved into a dirty, rat-infested one-bedroom apartment in Greenwich Village that he shared with a friend. The apartment's benefit was that it was affordable, and from there he continued trying to peddle his work to New York editors. This time it did not take long until he sold another cartoon to a magazine named *Judge*. The magazine was so impressed with Ted's work that he was offered a job as a writer and artist, for which he was paid $75 a week. The prospect of full-time work was all that Ted and Helen needed to move ahead with their plans. They were married on November 29, 1927.

After a brief honeymoon Ted was back at work at *Judge*, and he threw himself into the magazine with the same vigor he had displayed at *Jack-O-Lantern*. Ted had many ideas for humorous cartoons, and he set to work putting them down. He took to signing all his work with "Seuss," and shortly thereafter he added the "Dr." to make up for the graduate degree he did not receive from Oxford. Ted later said that he did not want to use the name Geisel, because he was "saving it for the Great American Novel" he intended to write.

The newly wed couple moved into a rather decrepit apartment on New York's west side, but that did not prevent Ted and Helen from enjoying married life. They took in all that the city had to offer with its parties, fine restaurants, and shows and plays on Broadway, and slowly Ted began to build a following of readers in *Judge*. Other magazines, including *Life* and *Vanity Fair*, were starting to request cartoons by Dr. Seuss as well. One of the fans who wrote to *Judge* asking for an original Dr. Seuss cartoon was Theodore Roosevelt Jr., the son of the man who had crushed young Ted's spirit at the Boy Scout award ceremony so many years earlier.

At about this same time, Ted's career was about to take an entirely different turn.

"Quick, Henry, the Flit!"

While preparing a cartoon that showed an armored knight using a bug sprayer to kill insects, Ted opted to use the name Flit, one of two rival sprays of the time, on the sprayer. The cartoon—and Flit's name—was seen by the wife of one the spray-maker's advertising executives. She urged her husband to contact Ted, and the result was an advertising campaign that produced one of the best-known lines ever: "Quick, Henry, the Flit!" It was also the first major advertising campaign developed using humorous cartoons.

The phrase became famous, and soon Ted's work was appearing in newspapers and billboards around the country. Flit sales exploded, and Ted began work on what would eventually become a 17-year relationship with the company that made the spray, Standard Oil of New Jersey. In addition to his Flit illustrations, Ted drew monsters for ads for the motor oil branch of Standard Oil. These creatures included the Moto-Raspus, the Moto-

Munchus, and the Karbo-Nockus, drawings that some commentators have observed were the forerunners of the fantastical beings that would later turn up in Ted's children's books.

Ted's work with Standard Oil brought him a new measure of freedom and the time to pursue both his writing and his drawing. Because the season for selling bug spray was short—confined mainly to the summer months—Ted and Helen also had time off to travel. One of the trips they took was to the town of La Jolla, located in southern California, just north of San Diego. The young couple immediately fell in love with the beautiful ocean vistas and calm pace, especially when compared with their hectic lives back in New York. They agreed that they would purchase a small place in La Jolla as soon as they could.

Meanwhile, Ted was still churning out work for *Judge.* A cover he drew for the magazine in the spring of 1929 is an early indicator of what was to come. It featured animals such as a hippopotamus, turtle, and an antlered dog that were similar to creatures that would later turn up in his children's books. Later that same year, the United States experienced an economic event that would send the country into a downward spiral for many years. On October 28, 1929, the stock market crashed. This was the beginning of the Great Depression, and although it would cripple much of the country, Ted and Helen, like many other artists and entertainers of the period, were not hurt as much as other people. Even in bad times, the public still wanted to laugh and be entertained.

Ted continued his work for other Standard Oil products, and his reputation in advertising grew. At the same time, he continued with his drawings. He and Helen moved into an apartment on Park Avenue, and despite the country's difficulties, life was looking good for the Geisels.

Welcome to *Mulberry Street*

The year 1931 was marked by bad and good events for Ted, who was just 27 years old. Tragically, that year Ted's mother died unexpectedly from an inoperable brain tumor. But in that same year Ted made his first foray into children's books, when an editor for Viking Press contacted him about illustrating a humor collection for young boys. The book had originally been published in Britain, and Ted's drawings helped the American edition sell very well, propelling it onto *The New York Times* best-seller list and spawning a follow-up title. Critics praised the books, and Ted's success inspired him to work on a children's ABC book on his own, which, despite the introduction of such creatures as a long-necked whizzleworp and a green-striped cholmondelet, was rejected by all the publishers to whom he presented it.

Meanwhile, Ted continued his career in advertising. His cartooning for magazines slowed, but his list of ad clients grew. Ted's work schedule allowed him plenty of time to do what he wanted, and he and Helen traveled extensively, as Ted filled notebook after notebook with his sketches. By the time the couple had been married nine years, they had traveled to 30 different countries around the globe. But it was a trip to Europe aboard the H.M.S. *Kungsholm* in the summer of 1936 that was to change Ted's future for good. The mood across the continent was serious, as Germany's Adolf Hitler seemed on the verge of launching into war.

On the *Kungsholm* headed for home, the ocean did not provide any calming effect. Rough seas violently tossed the ship back and forth, and Ted spent much of the trip hunkered down listening to the rhythm of the ship's engines as it tried to beat the tough weather. The sound of those machines stuck in his head, and Ted furiously scribbled some notes that included an image of a "horse and wagon," as he tried to make sense of what he had written. Even back on land, Ted could not get the sound of those engines out of his head, and returning to his notes he started writing a story set to their rhythm. One of the lines he had jotted down, "And to think that I saw it on Mulberry Street," stayed with him.

However, the rest of the story did not come easily for Ted. He wrote and rewrote the tale of Marco, a young boy whose wild imagination outpaces the ordinary street scenes he sees. Ted compulsively reworked his illustrations—a trait that would define his work in the years to come. When he was stuck or uncertain how to proceed, Helen oversaw him, reading and questioning Ted about every facet of the story.

When he finished *And to Think That I Saw It on Mulberry Street* six months later, Ted began showing it to publishers around the city. But despite his considerable fame as a cartoonist, an ad illustrator, and, more recently, a children's book illustrator, no one took any interest in his title. Twenty-seven publishers in all rejected his book. Editors around the city had different reasons for turning down his book. Some said that it was too different from other children's titles. Others said that the book lacked a clear message for young readers. Regardless of their reasons, their criticism and rejection stung Ted.

The Right Side of the Street

After months of trying unsuccessfully to interest publishers in *And to Think That I Saw It on Mulberry Street*, Ted had all but given up on writing children's books, when he ran into an old classmate from Dartmouth, Mike McClintock. The two men nearly bumped into one another as they happened down the same side of a busy New York street. McClintock had recently become an editor at Vanguard Press, and he was looking for new children's book authors. Ted, who had just come from his final unsuccessful meeting with a publisher, was carrying his book under his arm.

Within an hour, McClintock had Ted back at his office, where he met Vanguard's president, who agreed to publish the title. Once again, Ted had been in the right place at the right time. "If I had been going down the other side of Madison Avenue," he later told his biographers, "I'd be in the dry-cleaning business today."

From the start, Ted—now about to become even more widely known as Dr. Seuss—was incredibly fussy about what went into his books. From the words to the colors, the artist knew exactly what he wanted. But as soon as *And to Think That I Saw It on Mulberry Street* hit bookshelves, it was clear that Ted's fastidiousness would pay off. Critics raved about the book, and small reviews in *The New Yorker* and *The New York Times* bolstered sales of the book.

But it was clear that Dr. Seuss's work did not fit with the stories produced by other children's authors. For one, Ted's stories lent equal importance to pictures as well as to words. He wanted young readers to be able to figure out the story even if they could not read all the words. This approach won many fans. Beatrix Potter, who wrote the *Peter Rabbit* books, called *And to Think That I Saw It on Mulberry Street* "the cleverest book I have met with for many years." But despite the book's quick success, Ted realized that writing children's stories was a tough way to make a living. After six years in publication Ted's first book earned less than $4,000. Still, Dr. Seuss was on his way to becoming a hero to young readers—and their parents.

Hundreds of Hats and Chrysanthemum-Pearl

Now, with one successful children's title published, Vanguard Press was asking Ted for another. Ted was still gaining his feet as a children's author. "I knew nothing about children's books," he later admitted. But he understood the timeless appeal of fairy tales, and that, coupled with Ted's own collection of hats, fed his imagination for his second children's title, *The 500 Hats of Bartholomew Cubbins.*

Like *And to Think That I Saw It on Mulberry Street*, the new book quickly became a success, but Dr. Seuss was not necessarily at ease with his newfound fame. Demands on the new author required that he appear in front of crowds, and when Ted was asked to speak to a crowd at the New York Public Library after the release of *And to Think That I Saw It on Mulberry Street,* his stage fright surfaced. As Ted approached the library at the time of his appearance, he could not bring himself to go inside. Instead he hid outside the building and never made his appointment.

The same scenario played itself out again with the release of *The 500 Hats of Bartholomew Cubbins.* After accepting an engagement to speak at a women's college just outside of New York City, the college called Helen at home to ask where Ted was when his appointed speaking

Ted strikes a comical pose near a sculpture of one of his creations. (Time Life Pictures/Getty Images)

time came and went. When Ted returned home that evening, he told Helen that he had gone as far as Grand Central Station to catch his train but no farther. With the thought of appearing in front of a crowd filling his head, he had spent the rest of the afternoon hiding out in the station.

Ted's stage fright was not the only issue plaguing the fledgling author. *The 500 Hats* was dedicated to Chrysanthemum-Pearl, a child Ted had come to mention often. When friends of the Geisels mentioned their children, Ted would brag about the accomplishments of his and Helen's child, Chrysanthemum-Pearl. But like Ted's other creations, Chrysanthemum was only a product of his imagination. The Geisels never had children of their own.

Much has been made of the fact that Dr. Seuss, the world's most famous children's author, did not have kids of his own. Some people have speculated that since Ted had no children he did not actually like kids. But that was not the truth. When asked why he had no children, Ted once said, "I don't think spending your days surrounded by kids is necessary to write the kind of books I write. . . . Once a writer starts talking down to kids, he's lost. Kids can pick up on that kind of thing." The truth was that Ted and Helen wanted children of their own, but a medical condition prevented the couple from having them. Instead, they made up for the absence with fanciful creations like Chrysanthemum-Pearl, and the childlike qualities to which Ted clung throughout his life.

The Not-So-Great Invention

In 1939 a World's Fair was held in New York City. Ted had been anticipating the arrival of the fair for some time. For nearly a year he and many others had been at work on an invention they were sure would make them wealthy beyond their wildest dreams. The economy had not yet completely righted itself, and although Ted had not suffered much compared to many others, it had still been a time of belt-tightening for everyone.

Ted's invention, the Infantograph, was first conceived late in 1938. Ted had imagined a machine that would produce a picture of what a couple's future child would look like were they to get pregnant. The machine would work by taking a side-by-side picture of a man and a woman, combining that photograph and superimposing it over the face of an infant. To complete the project, Ted partnered with a couple of other inventors. But, as the World's Fair neared, it became clear that the device could not be made to work. The children all came out looking strange, some of them appearing with a moustache if the male in the original photograph happened to have one. While Ted remained fond of the idea for years to come, it never came to fruition. (However, a similar device would eventually surface—55 years later.)

If the Infantograph hinted that Ted was not concerned with children's books alone, *The Seven Lady Godivas*, Ted's next book, proved the point. It was Ted's first—and, for the most part, his last—venture into adult books. Although it was an illustrated story, the book was written and drawn for adults. It was also a complete flop. The book was released by a new publisher, Random House, headed by Bennett Cerf. Ted had met Cerf before he completed *The 500 Hats*, and Cerf was certain that he wanted to publish Ted's books. First, however, Ted had to fulfill his obligations to Vanguard Press. But when Ted told Cerf about his idea for *The Seven Lady Godivas*, the Random House head jumped at the opportunity—so long as he could publish the other books Ted would write as well.

The Seven Lady Godivas was soon forgotten, and Ted was at work on another book for young readers, *The King's Stilts*. Like *The 500 Hats of Bartholomew Cubbins*, it was a fairy tale, and it is the first title in which Helen's assistance was crucial to Ted finishing the story. Throughout the process, she helped him with the words and plot or anywhere he was having a problem. "Helen was an editor and a partner," Ted later said. In fact, he added years later, some of the lines that appeared in his stories were words Helen had written. Although *The King's Stilts* was not very successful either, Cerf and Random House continued to throw their support behind Ted.

A New Story Is Hatched

Despite the many books he wrote and illustrated, writing was not always an easy task for Ted. His characters and

Throughout his career, Ted worked tirelessly on one project after another. (Time Life Pictures/Getty Images)

stories often developed over a long period of time, and first drafts would appear as sketches, with the words coming later. The words would then go through several revisions as the story unfolded, often over a period of months.

But sometimes Ted got lucky. One day while working on some sketches, Ted left a couple drawings on his desk while he went out for a walk. While he was gone, a breeze stirred up the drawings, and one picture of an elephant fell on top of a picture of a tree so that when Ted returned, it looked as if the elephant was sitting in the tree. That led Ted to ask some questions about why an elephant would be up in a tree.

The resulting story, *Horton Hatches the Egg*, would be Dr. Seuss's most successful book to date. But even though the idea came by chance, writing it was not an easy task. The main character, an elephant named Horton, went through many changes, as did the lazy bird Mayzie, for whom Horton baby-sits an egg. In the book's grand finale, Horton's efforts produce a creature that is half bird, half elephant. Before Ted was finished, he would rewrite each character from top to bottom, and, as the deadline for the book drew near, Helen seemed to be more worried about its completion than Ted did.

For his part, Ted had taken up a new hobby: political cartooning. Hitler continued to menace Europe, and Ted began sketching derogatory cartoons of the evil leader. It was Helen who largely completed the final lines of *Horton Hatches the Egg*, in which the elephant-bird is hatched, Ted later admitted. But regardless of who did the work, Bennett Cerf was thrilled at the imaginative new title.

From its initial publication, *Horton Hatches the Egg* was a hit. The dedicated elephant was Ted's most complete creation. Gone was the fairy-tale style that Ted had employed in *The 500 Hats of Bartholomew Cubbins* and *The King's Stilts*. In their place was a story grown entirely from imagination, one that would set a tone for Dr. Seuss's future titles. Horton was a human animal with shortcomings, desires, and, perhaps most important, morality: "I meant what I said, and I said what I meant . . . / An elephant's faithful—one hundred per cent!" reads the book's most famous line.

Horton Hatches the Egg was notable for other reasons as well. The animals in the book—Horton, Mayzie, the moose, lion, and others—were, for the most part, recognizable as a particular type of animal, even if they were drawn according to Ted's original style. But the appearance of the elephant-bird at the end of the story gave rise to a new facet of Ted's books: the imaginary, fantastical Seussian creature, the animal that was part one thing and part something else. The book also contained another feature that would become standard in Ted's work: a particular rhythm of words that would eventually lead to completely made-up language in future books. *Horton Hatches the Egg* defined the path down which Dr. Seuss was headed.

After a couple of books that had failed to generate the excitement of his *And to Think That I Saw It on Mulberry Street* debut, Dr. Seuss's reputation was again on the rise. Ted was sure of what he wanted to be: a children's book author. But first, World War II would intervene, and Ted would quit writing children's books for seven years.

4

FILMMAKING IN WORLD WAR II

By 1940 Ted had explored several career paths. From his days at Oxford when he thought he would be an English professor to a long stint as an ad man for Standard Oil, the 36-year-old artist had tried a number of different things, many of which he liked. But it was not until he began writing and illustrating children's books that he felt certain about what he wanted to do. Even though *Horton Hatches the Egg* had shown Ted an occupation, he was not about to give up habits such as cartooning. Ted's cartoons of Hitler and the global political situation caught the eye of the publisher of New York's tabloid newspaper, *PM*. After his first cartoon was printed in the paper, Ted was asked for more. Many years would pass before Dr. Seuss would write children's books again.

No world event had inspired in Ted the fervor that the war being waged in Europe inspired. "I had no great causes or interest in social issues until Hitler," he said. But when he took up the cause of World War II, he did so with the energy of one truly committed to a cause. At the time when the war was largely concentrated in Europe, many Americans were resistant to the United States' involvement in it.

But Ted was a vocal—and insistent—critic of Hitler, Italian dictator Benito Mussolini, and American citizens and politicians who spoke out against U.S. involvement in the conflict. Ted's incisive cartoons criticized personalities such as Charles Lindbergh, considered an American hero for his daring trans-Atlantic flight, who called for neutrality in the war.

Ted liked these cartoons because he felt they provided him an opportunity for complete honesty. Although he would later look back on these drawings as "shoddy," they provided him a chance to take a stand for a cause long before America was finally pulled into the war, following the bombing of Pearl Harbor on December 7, 1941. Ted's cartoons continued to draw praise from supporters who believed his point of view and criticism from those who thought that Ted had pulled the country into war because of his outspoken viewpoint. Some people even claimed that Ted could afford to be outspoken because after years

... and the Wolf chewed up the children and spit out their bones ...
But those were <u>Foreign Children</u> and it really didn't matter."

During World War II, Ted spoke out against Hitler, Mussolini, and other leaders in a series of political cartoons. (Associated Press)

of cartooning, he was now 38 years old—too old to be drafted into the war.

Ted Enlists

But in the fall of 1942 Ted proved his detractors wrong and applied to join the navy. However, before his application could be approved, he was asked to join the army's Signal Corps working for Academy Award–winning film director Frank Capra. The Geisels moved out of their New York apartment, and Captain Theodor Seuss Geisel was soon inducted into the Information and Education Division of the army.

Other artists and writers joined Capra's division, which was charged with making documentary films designed to boost the morale of U.S. soldiers. Although the unit did not have to undergo the typical rigors of an Army division, Ted and his fellow soldiers did have to complete field drills that usually proved to be his downfall. Athletically ill at ease since his youth, Ted was, one biographer noted, "hopelessly uncoordinated."

Capra's soldiers did not live on an army base, instead returning to their private homes at the end of each day. For Ted and Helen this was a house in the hills above Hollywood. During the day, while Ted was off soldiering, Helen took up writing children's books of her own such as *Tommy's Wonderful Rides* and *Bobby and His Airplane*. "She supported us during the war," Ted later told an interviewer at *Good Housekeeping* magazine. And when Ted was not involved in the war efforts, the couple explored their new home in Los Angeles.

Ted's work with Capra proved beneficial for the new recruit. Capra, who would go on to direct such films as *It's a Wonderful Life* and *Pocketful of Miracles,* helped Ted with concepts such as story and plot development. "[Capra] taught me conciseness, and I learned a lot about the juxtaposition of words and visual images," Ted later said of his mentor. It was here that Ted would learn the art of animation, as Capra's unit assembled animated training films for U.S. troops. But Ted quickly tired of such work, and Capra put the artist to work on a new project—including a secret film project intended for the victorious American soldiers who would be occupying Germany after the Nazis were defeated.

Titled *Your Job in Germany,* the film Ted worked on had to be shown to all the field officers commanding the war, and Ted had to travel to Europe to win their approval for his work. With a couple other soldiers Ted traveled around France, Belgium, Luxembourg, and the Netherlands, but during a brief trip into the town of Bastogne in Belgium, Ted was trapped behind enemy lines for three days after fighting flared up once again.

Back in the States Ted worked on other film projects, but with the surrender of Japan in August 1945 Ted's military service was coming to an end. However, the end of the war was met with personal tragedy just a month later when Ted's sister, Marnie, died of a heart attack at age 43. Ted was shattered by the news and never publicly commented on his only sibling's untimely death. In January 1946 Ted was released from his military duty, earning the Legion of Merit award for his informational training films.

Hollywood Woes

Your Job in Germany proved to be an inspirational film, particularly to Warner Brothers studio head Jack Warner, who after seeing the movie secured its civilian rights and remade it into the documentary *Hitler Lives?* Although Ted did not receive credit for Warner's remake, *Hitler Lives?* won the 1946 Academy Award for best documentary short subject, and Ted was signed to a $500-a-week contract with another producer. However, that relationship did not last long. After working on a screen treatment based on the book *Rebel Without a Cause*—which would later be developed into the film of the same name starring James Dean—Ted's work was discarded when he and the producer could not agree on what to include in the synopsis.

Ted next went to work adapting another wartime film titled *Your Job in Japan*. Similar to his earlier movie concerning the vanquished German foes, an American studio wanted a stateside version of the *Japan* film and requested that Ted work on it. He enlisted Helen in the project, and together they wrote *Design for Death*, a 48-minute documentary that underwent more than 30 major revisions and prolonged battles with a producer who wanted to insert footage of tanks rolling through a montage of 16th-century Japan. Typical of Ted's support of the underdog, his and Helen's film depicted a Japanese people who had been held captive by their rulers for centuries. *Design for Death* won the 1947 Academy Award for best documentary feature, and Ted and Helen attended that year's ceremony at the Shrine Auditorium in Los Angeles.

While Ted had mixed success in Hollywood, he missed the world of books. But even as he moved back to writing, he found it difficult to break his ties to Hollywood completely. When he was asked to write a new animation feature for one studio, he turned in *Gerald McBoing-Boing*, the story of a boy who can only speak in sounds. The film won an Academy Award—the third for which Ted had been primarily responsible—for best cartoon in 1951.

Ted's filmmaking continued that year. A large monetary advance convinced Ted to start work on a full-length feature titled *The 5,000 Fingers of Dr. T*, the story of a young boy who revolts against the tyrannical Dr. Terwilliker. Dr. T is an evil musician who forces his child protégés into an endless piano recital. For Ted the movie was an opportunity to bring the ideas expressed in his books—the idea of the underdog standing up against his oppressor—to the big screen. "[Ted] desperately wanted to be a success in films," an acquaintance of Ted's later told his biographers.

The Geisels moved back to Hollywood from La Jolla. Helen was not crazy about Ted's pursuit of the project—especially since he was sacrificing time that he could have spent writing a book—but as usual her support of Ted was unconditional. The making of a feature film, however, may have been more than Ted bargained for. As the production was delayed and script changes became more than Ted could handle, he and the film's producer did what they could to preserve the original idea.

The making of the film dragged on one, then two years. When the film was finally shown for an advance audience in January 1953, the crowd began walking out shortly after the movie began. "It was a disaster," Ted later said. "Careers were ruined." Shortly thereafter the Geisels left for an extended trip in Japan, just as *The 5,000 Fingers* was hitting theaters. But when they returned home they found that the reviews for the movie were not all bad. Some critics appreciated what the filmmakers had tried to do, and a reviewer in *The New York Times* noted the movie's "good intentions." Although Ted considered *The 5,000 Fingers* a blight on his resume and refused to discuss it in later years, history vindicated the picture. The movie became a fan favorite in the video era, as film buffs grew to appreciate its dark satire and the film's blend of cartoon and live action.

A scene from The 5,000 Fingers of Dr. T, *for which Ted wrote the screenplay.* (Associated Press)

5

TURTLES, SNEETCHES, AND OTHER GREAT CREATURES

Seven years had passed since Ted had written a children's book, and when he emerged from the army he was ready to get back to work. Advances in printing techniques allowed Ted access to a variety of colors he had not been able to imagine with his earlier books, and Random House's Bennett Cerf was eager to get his best-selling author back to work. When the Geisels were ready to leave their temporary Hollywood residence, they were offered brief residence at the Los Angeles home of some friends. While there, Ted began painting illustrations for what would become *McElligot's Pool*, his first title since *Horton Hatches the Egg*.

When *McElligot's Pool* came out in 1947, Ted received his first nomination for a Caldecott Award, an honor handed out by the American Library Association to the artists of the best picture books for children. This book also continued the parade of imaginary creatures Ted had begun with *Horton*'s elephant-bird: This pool contained fish that were part cow and part kangaroo, in addition to having other nonaquatic features (such as a fish that released flowers in bloom). It was another step down a path that continued to veer further into Ted's wildly original imagination.

The Origin of Ideas

The years immediately following World War II became a fertile period for Ted. After *McElligot's Pool*, he completed several books in rapid succession, beginning with *Thidwick the Big-Hearted Moose*. The story of a generous moose whose antlers are overrun by an array of unwanted forest creatures, the book ends when Thidwick's antlers fall off and the animals living in them are turned into trophies. This sort of poetic justice would become increasingly common in Ted's work. "I shall never cease to wonder at these figments of your inexhaustible brain," Ted's editor at Random House wrote to him.

The editor was not the only person who wondered where Dr. Seuss's ideas originated. It was a question commonly posed to Ted who, with his standard wit, often said that he found his ideas "out in left field." Other times he said that he traveled to an Arizona desert where he got ideas from a retired thunderbird and that once a year he also went to a small town in Switzerland called Zybilknov, where he would have his cuckoo clock fixed. "While I am waiting for my clock, I walk the streets of the village and talk to some of its strange inhabitants. That is where I get the ideas for the characters in my books," he said.

Of course, nothing was further from the truth. Ted's ideas came from a variety of experiences, usually things that he had encountered during his own travels. For example, *Bartholomew and the Oobleck,* the book that followed *Thidwick the Big-Hearted Moose,* drew on an experience Ted had had while trapped in Luxembourg at the end of World War II. Published in 1949, *Bartholomew and the Oobleck* found Ted returning to the same Bartholomew that he had used 11 years earlier in *The 500 Hats of Bartholomew Cubbins.* In the new story, however, Bartholomew's king complains incessantly about the weather regardless of whether it's sunny or snowy or raining, until one day green goo begins to cover his kingdom. Ted later said that the story was inspired by a conversation between American soldiers he had overheard in Luxembourg.

"Rain, always rain!" one soldier said to the other. "Why can't we have something different for a change?"

Ted had filed their words away until they took shape in his story several years later. But he had been doing that all his life, reaching back to his childhood for characters and ideas that drove his stories. His next book, *If I Ran the Zoo*, appeared in 1950, and while some commentators believe it related to Ted's early trips to the Springfield zoo, he later said that the book was written in memory of his mother, who had been writing her own zoo story when he returned from Oxford years earlier.

Regardless of its origin, the story of Gerald McGrew was Ted's cleanest break from reality, in that it presented a menagerie of fantastical creatures such as the It-Kutch, Nerkle, and Seersucker that could only have come from one mind: Dr. Seuss's. But the animals were not the only inventions in *If I Ran the Zoo*. Ted created countries such as "Ka-Troo," and he seemed to be developing his own rhythmic language. It was a trademark by which all his future books would come to be defined.

California for Good

After Ted and Helen's extended stay in California through World War II, the couple had decided that they just could not return to New York. For one thing, Ted longed for a more moderate climate. They had spent enough time in

La Jolla to know that they wanted to live there, and in 1948 they bought an observation tower on two acres of land overlooking the Pacific Ocean. The tower had become something of a romantic getaway for young couples who had covered the inside with drawings of hearts and their initials, some of which Ted and Helen left when they redecorated the building.

After buying the property, the Geisels promptly sold the house they had been living at in Hollywood and began readying their new place. The tower rose 800 feet above the rest of the town, and from it Ted and Helen could see south to Mexico and north all the way to Los Angeles. The building, which became a landmark for local residents and visitors alike, became known as the Tower. At first Ted's studio was located upstairs with a commanding view of the Pacific Ocean. But Ted actually turned his desk away from the view so that he could concentrate on his work.

Even as Ted continued to turn out books—and movie projects—in the years after the war, he also kept up his work in advertising. Although he did not go out of his way to line up work with advertisers, some found their way to him, including Ford Motor Company, for which he helped develop ad ideas even as he completed *Bartholomew and the Oobleck.* Helen once said of his work habits, "He has the endurance of 40 buffaloes and thinks he can work day and night," but the truth was that Ted was stretching himself thin. He longed to focus on his children's books and put the rest of his work behind him. That is exactly what he suggested when he met with his agent Phyllis Jackson in 1953.

At the meeting Ted asked her whether she thought he could give up everything else, stay in La Jolla and write his books, and still earn $5,000 a year—an amount that he thought would provide him a comfortable living at that time. A friend reminded him that screenwriters earned five times as much money as that, but Ted said he did not expect to get rich writing children's books.

Ted and Helen took to their new life in La Jolla, involving themselves in community activities. One of these community functions, the drive to keep La Jolla free from commercial billboards and signs, would end up costing Ted some work. In an effort to persuade the town council to ban billboards from the sides of roads, Ted produced a pamphlet that made fun of two fictional characters, Guss and Zaxx, each of whom tried to create more signs than the other. The pamphlet helped win over the town council, which banned business billboards in La Jolla, but a sugar company that had hired Ted to design its signs promptly canceled its contract with him.

At the Tower, the couple hosted dinners for all sorts of people, including scientists, businesspeople, and other

Ted and Helen outside of their home in La Jolla, California.
(Getty Images)

writers and occasionally joined some of their new friends on short trips into nearby Mexico. Aside from these functions, Ted still valued his privacy and threw himself into his children's books with renewed vigor. He often worked late into the night and would start again early in the morning, spending 15 or 16 hours a day in his studio. He wrote best late at night, he said.

In 1953, at the urging of an editor at Random House, Ted returned to the elephant Horton, a character he had created 13 years earlier and nearly 3,000 miles away—back in New York—for *Horton Hears a Who!* Ted's inspiration for the story had grown out of a trip he and Helen had taken to Japan following the end of World War II. The main idea behind the new *Horton* title was revealed in one sentence that appeared several times in the story: "A person's a person. No matter how small."

In *Horton Hears a Who!*, the Whos are tiny creatures living on a speck of dust whose civilization is threatened when the dust nears a pool of water. Horton saves the Whos from the water and later from other animals in the jungle, including a band of monkeys named the Wickersham brothers—a name Ted borrowed from some Springfield neighbors of his childhood. With the book, Ted continued building on the themes of equality and generosity that he had begun with *Horton Hatches the Egg* and continued in *Thidwick the Big-Hearted Moose*. In January 1954 the Geisels delivered the manuscript for *Horton Hears a Who!* to Random House in New York, where the book was deemed a surefire success.

Praise and Illness

That May the Geisels were in good spirits. The article in *Life* magazine that suggested Ted was an author who could better children's reading primers had appeared, which would eventually lead Ted to write *The Cat in the Hat*. But he and Helen were quietly celebrating another triumph that, for the time being, they were keeping to themselves: They were about to embark on a trip to Ted's alma mater,

Dartmouth, where he would receive an honorary doctorate degree. Ted really would be Dr. Seuss.

Before they could leave for Dartmouth, however, Helen fell ill. Her mysterious condition quickly deteriorated as her entire body became paralyzed. It was a devastating blow for Ted, who had counted on Helen for so many years to take care of him. She was placed in a hospital in San Diego, and Ted stayed by her bedside for weeks. Their trip to Dartmouth had to be postponed as Helen's health worsened. But by late June she slowly began to recover. Although Helen would ultimately recover the use of her body, after her initial illness she never completely returned to the health she had enjoyed before.

That summer *Horton Hears a Who!* was released to unanimous praise. Among other things, the book was hailed as a critique of racism for its message of defending all persons. Another book, *On Beyond Zebra*, quickly followed, in which Ted stretched the alphabet to include new letters such as "Yuzz" and "Vroo." *On Beyond Zebra* also continued Ted's wordplay and rhyme schemes, and he dedicated the book to Helen. The following May, in 1955, the Geisels were able to make the trip to Dartmouth for the graduation ceremony.

The Year of the Cat—and the Grinch

As Ted worked on *The Cat in the Hat* through much of 1956 and into 1957, he had no idea that his newest character, the Cat, would eventually become his most popular. The Cat was a bit different from the other main characters Ted had created. The Cat was shrewd and, even though he did not intend to be, something of a troublemaker.

When Ted finally finished _The Cat in the Hat_ after more than a year—he originally thought he could write the book in a couple weeks—he was relieved. He had invested much more in the book than he had thought necessary, but the book's instant success proved to be worth it. However, Ted had other projects he was committed to. One idea, the commercialization of Christmas, was a subject Ted had been concerned with for years. This was the basis for the other title he completed in 1957, _How the Grinch Stole Christmas!_

For this story, Ted returned to the creatures called the Whos, whom he had created a couple of years earlier for _Horton Hears a Who!_ In the story, the Grinch is jealous of the way in which the Whos celebrate Christmas, so he steals all their presents, hoping to ruin the day. When that doesn't work, the Grinch has a change of heart and returns everything to the little Whos, even going so far as to celebrate with them. _How the Grinch Stole Christmas!_ also would become one of Dr. Seuss's most popular books, but Ted later admitted that finishing this title was not easy either. He said that he was not quite sure how to end the book and that he "had gone through thousands of . . .

Ted's How the Grinch Stole Christmas! *has become a holiday favorite of children and adults everywhere.* (Photofest)

choices" before he settled on the final ending for *How the Grinch Stole Christmas!*

For Ted, however, it was a typical way in which he proceeded through a book. He would begin his stories with a situation or conflict and then write himself into a corner so that there did not appear to be a way in which to end the book. "People who think about the endings first come up with inferior products," he later told his biographers.

Following the success of *The Cat in the Hat, Grinch* was an immediate hit. Ted was becoming increasingly famous, as more and more people discovered Dr. Seuss's books. The books were starting to come faster. In 1958 Ted wrote two new books: *The Cat in the Hat Comes Back!* and *Yertle the Turtle and Other Stories.* The second Cat in the Hat book was another title for his and Phyllis Cerf's new line, Beginner Books.

Beginner Books

Ted and Helen had been devoting a lot of time to the imprint Beginner Books, which had been launched after *The Cat in the Hat.* The idea behind these books was to further the mission that Ted had started with *The Cat in the Hat*: He wanted to produce interesting and exciting books for very young readers—different from the traditional learning-to-read titles that he thought failed to inspire them. Ted wanted strong stories with strong illustrations;

he thought every page should end with a cliffhanger so that the young reader would feel compelled to turn the page. And he despised using anything formulaic to tell his stories. "I try to treat the child as an equal and go on the assumption a child can understand anything that is read to him if the writer takes care to state it *clearly* and *simply* enough," Ted told one interviewer.

With his strong feelings as to what made a good children's title, he and Helen and Phyllis began trying to work with other authors to expand the Beginner Books series into a larger line. But Ted quickly found that very few authors could create the kind of book he wanted. For Ted, writing a children's book could take between 12 and 18 months, and for a book 60 pages long he might draw as many as 500 pictures—most of which would go in the trash. The same was true of the words. He could write 1,000 pages of words, even though most of them wouldn't be used. "I realize [my books] look as if they've been put together in 23 seconds," he said. "But 99 percent of what I do ends up in the scrap basket."

Still, the new series of books needed authors other than Ted in order to be successful. Random House had invested a good deal of money to get the company up and running, but Ted and Phyllis clashed early on as to what sort of books would be acceptable. Despite the back-and-forth bickering between Ted on the West Coast and Phyllis in New

York, Beginner Books continued to prosper. Random House eventually purchased the entire company and rewarded the Geisels with generous stock shares in the company.

Ted Takes a Stand

Even though Ted's career was providing him with a sizable income, the concept of money bored him as it always had—so much so that he rarely even carried cash. Ted's thoughts were with his work, and through the late 1950s this continued unabated.

With *Yertle the Turtle*, which was a parable of Adolf Hitler's life, Ted returned to the politicizing he had practiced in the newspaper *PM*. But up to this point in his career, it was one of the only places Ted thought that he had offered an overt moral. While Ted believed that his stories were positive and could be interpreted in certain ways, he resisted the idea that he was trying to push a moral agenda on young readers. "Kids gag at having morals crammed down their throats," he told one interviewer. Any story that has a dramatic point also contained a moral, he added, but "I never set out to prove a point."

Whatever Ted's approach, it was working with readers of all stripes. At the end of 1958 Ted was touring the country, promoting both *Yertle the Turtle* and *The Cat in the Hat Comes Back!* Teachers and librarians scrambled to get the crowd-shy Dr. Seuss into their classrooms and facilities.

Ted appeared at zoos and accepted awards, and his books continued to fly off the shelves. But that did not make the process of writing any easier. Ted still struggled to perfect each word, each sentence, and each page. And when he created something that he was satisfied with, he made sure that his work was printed exactly to his specifications. This was particularly evident on one of his Beginner Books, *One Fish, Two Fish, Red Fish, Blue Fish*.

When Ted met with the publisher's production department to discuss *One Fish, Two Fish, Red Fish, Blue Fish*, he took along three uncommon crayon colors that he demanded the publishers reproduce for his book. Given the printing technology available at the time, matching colors in such a way was an incredibly difficult task. But Ted was not satisfied until the colors were printed exactly as he wanted to see them, which they were when the book was printed in 1960. With *The Cat in the Hat Comes Back!*, Ted ordered that a new book jacket be made because he felt one line was too dark—even though the book had already sold 100,000 copies.

Not Your Typical Children's Book

Ted continued to challenge conventional ideas about children's literature. His stories are full of characters who behave badly, only to be redeemed in the end. In *How the Grinch Stole Christmas!*, for example, at the start of the story the Grinch's heart is two sizes too small. But by the end of the tale his heart has swelled to three times its original size. The Cat in the Hat is mischievous, and it seems certain that he will get his two young friends in trouble. However, the Cat ends up saving the day—and the children have fooled their mother.

Dr. Seuss's books were marked by other features as well. Ted continued to push the envelope of taste where he thought he could get away with it. In *Yertle the Turtle*, one character "burps"; it was the first time that word had been used in a children's story. And Ted's story continued in the Seussian verse and rhythms he had established early in his career. With the exception of three early titles—*The 500 Hats of Bartholomew Cubbins*, *The King's Stilts*, and *Bartholomew and the Oobleck*—all of Ted's books were written in his particular rhyme scheme. "Rhyming forces recognition of words. You also establish a rhythm, and that tends to make kids want to go on. If you break the rhythm, a child feels unfulfilled," Ted later said.

Ted's formula was working. By the spring of 1960, five of the top 16 best-selling children's books were Ted's. But as Ted's career grew increasingly successful with Beginner Books and his other titles, Helen's health worsened. She continued to aid Ted as an editor, bookkeeper, and confidante, but the growing workload demanded of Dr. Seuss was taking its toll on his wife. The tension became particularly acute when Ted neared the end of a book. Helen described the scene to a journalist: "About two weeks before the completion of every book, [Ted] seems to go into a tailspin, decides that nothing in the book is any good, that he can't possibly finish it, and . . . I have a great job to do in keeping everything from falling into the scrap basket."

A $50 Bet

Ted was about to write his most popular title, which would also be one of his briefest. *Green Eggs and Ham*, which was published as a Beginner Book, came about as a wager from Random House's Bennett Cerf to Ted. Cerf bet Ted $50 that he could not write a book using only 50 words. It was the same sort of trial that had sparked *The Cat in the Hat*, and Ted, never one to shy away from a challenge, began to work. When he was finished, Ted had created another rambunctious character in the memorable Sam-I-am, who implores an anonymous counterpart to taste the stomach-turning dish.

Among the book's lasting effects would be countless platters of green eggs, served to Ted at many, many functions, and even more attempts to pin a specific meaning on Ted's short tale. But on this account he held fast to his rejection of particular messages. "I seldom start with [a moral message], but when you write a kid's book, somebody's got to win," he said. "You find yourself preaching in spite of yourself. But sometimes people find morals where there are none. People have read all kinds of things into *Green Eggs and Ham*, including biblical connotations. . . . I'm getting blamed for a lot of stuff I haven't done."

In 1961 Ted finished another of his "big books," *The Sneetches and Other Stories*. He followed it with Dr. Seuss's *Sleep Book*, which would be the last "big book" Ted would write for several years. Instead, he turned his full attention toward the Beginner series, and the production of a succession of titles including *Hop on Pop* and *Dr. Seuss's ABC* (both published in 1963), and *Fox in Socks*, which arrived in 1965. Beginner Books was publishing a number of other authors as well by this time, and it fell on Ted and Helen to edit and approve their work. The friction between Ted and Phyllis Cerf continued, until eventually Phyllis left Beginner and Ted assumed the lead role at the imprint.

Despite the dizzying workload, Ted and Helen maintained an active social life that included plenty of travel and entertaining. Many of their friends taught at nearby University of California San Diego and included other couples such as Audrey and Grey Dimond, whom the Geisels met in 1960. The couples became fast friends, often traveling to parties together.

TV and a Terrible Turn

Despite Ted's previous experiences with the big screen on *The 5,000 Fingers of Dr. T*, Chuck Jones, a longtime friend who worked for MGM and whom Ted had served with in World War II, convinced the author that his stories would be perfect for television. Ted and Chuck set about preparing an animated TV version of *How the Grinch Stole Christmas!*, in time for the 1966 holiday season. *The Grinch* turned out to be one of the most expensive shows of its length ever produced—but audiences approved.

The show drove sales of the book, so much so that Ted and Chuck began work on an animated version of *Horton Hears a Who!* the following year, to coincide with Thanksgiving. Before the holiday, however, Ted would face perhaps the gravest tragedy of his life. On October 23, 1967, Helen Geisel was found dead in her bedroom. Apparently distraught about her own failing health and the burden she might place on Ted, she had ended her life with a handful of pills. Ted was crushed by Helen's death, and friends and associates gathered to console him. But despite the devastating news, he vowed that he would remain at the Tower in La Jolla and continue his work.

6

A MORAL TALE

While Helen's death proved an immeasurable tragedy in Ted's life, the author did the best he could to continue as he had before. And it soon became clear that Ted would not be alone for very long. The following summer he married Audrey Dimond, an old friend of his and Helen's. On August 5, 1968, the couple was married in Reno, Nevada. With the marriage Ted became a stepfather to Audrey's daughters, Lea Grey and Lark.

Ted also began limiting his trips to New York, as his editors from Random House instead came to La Jolla to meet with him. He started work on a new line of books called the Bright & Early Books, intended for children who had not yet started to read. The first of the new series was *The Foot Book*, praised upon its release in 1968. For Ted, helping the youngest children learn to read was one of the greatest rewards of his work.

Ted's star continued to rise with each successive book. And as he grew older—in 1968 Ted turned 64—the normally shy author began to open up. Some credited his new wife Audrey with the transformation, but whatever the reason, Ted started to make appearances at public-speaking engagements as well as agreeing to the occasional television interview.

But his work was keeping him busier than ever. By the end of the 1960s and the start of the new decade, Ted was juggling his work with Bright & Early Books, Beginner Books, and his "big books." In two years, between 1969 and 1970, he produced one big book, *I Can Lick 30 Tigers Today! and Other Stories*; one Beginner Book, *I Can Draw It Myself*; and one Bright & Early title, *Mr. Brown Can Moo! Can You?* But he was about to start work on a title that would come to define the final phase of Dr. Seuss's career and divide some of his fans and critics alike.

Taming the Smogulous Smoke

In 1956, Ted had produced a pamphlet titled *Signs of Civilization* for the La Jolla Town Council. The pamphlet decried the explosion of billboards around Ted's adopted hometown. He would return to that theme nearly a decade and half later, inspired by the population and construction boom in Southern California. As far as Ted was concerned, people just did not care much about the environment. Whether it was the eruption of signs or buildings cluttering the landscape, littering, lack of conservation, or other wasteful behaviors, Ted thought that it was time to say something about environmentalism.

One of his first goals in starting *The Lorax* was to write a book that was not dull or "full of statistics and preachy." And he made no excuses for what he was about to write. "It's one of the few things I ever set out to do that was straight propaganda," he told an interviewer many years later. Unfortunately, the story was not developing very well. Ted turned the idea over in his head, but it was not until a trip to Africa in the fall of 1970 that the idea would unveil itself to the author. One afternoon while on vacation, Ted saw a herd of elephants come up over the hill. The animals sparked something in him, and Ted grabbed the only thing near him that he had to write on—a laundry list. "I wrote 90 percent of the book that afternoon," he later said. "I got some kind of release watching those elephants."

When *The Lorax* was published in 1971, Ted made sure no one would mistake the message of its main character. The book blasted pollution and pointed a finger at greed and big business. Ted changed the colors he used in the book to a softer, more pastel palette, and he wrote some of his most imaginative descriptions ever—"smogulous smoke," for example. But the book failed to achieve the sales of most of his titles. Some readers did not like its

A scene from the animated version of The Lorax, *a story that Ted described as "straight propaganda" in favor of environmental awareness.* (Photofest)

message, and *The Lorax* arrived at a time in which the country had yet to grasp the seriousness of the environmental problem.

Although the book was made into a television special the following year, it wasn't until the 1980s that the book's message would take hold. Many years later, in 1989, the book would generate the greatest controversy of Ted's career when a campaign to remove the title from a school library raged in a northern California logging town. The book remained on shelves, but Ted was adamant about its message. "*The Lorax* doesn't say lumbering is immoral," he told his biographers. "I live in a house made of wood and write books printed on paper. It's a book about going easy on what we've got. It's antipollution and antigreed."

The Real Dr. Seuss

Despite Ted's steady output, he managed to get even busier as time went on. In addition to Dr. Seuss's three series for Random House, Ted eventually wrote more than a dozen books that he did not illustrate. Using the pseudonym Theodore LeSieg, Ted worked primarily with an illustrator named Roy McKie, although several other people illustrated LeSieg titles as well. Another book that Ted and Random House editor Mike Frith cowrote, *Because a Little Bug Went Ka-Choo*, was published in 1975 under the name "Rosetta Stone."

Elsewhere, Ted was giving up certain duties. Since Helen's death he had taken over her editorial duties for Beginner Books, but many of the series' other authors found it difficult to work with Ted. He was too focused on his work, they said, and he often lacked the subtlety required to work with other creative personalities. By 1973 he had turned over most of his duties for the line to editors at Random House's New York office.

As Ted moved into his seventies, he began experiencing health problems common to people of his age. But one such problem, which had crept up on him through the mid-1970s, suddenly caught him by surprise. Ted woke up and could not see. He had known that he was developing an eye condition called cataracts that clouds the eye's lens. He could not identify specific colors as well as he once was able to, and his drawings appeared "squiggly" and erratic to him. It was a terrific blow for a man who depended as much on his eyes as he did his hands. His condition was eventually corrected with surgery, but not before it inspired a title, *I Can Read With My Eyes Shut*—a book Ted dedicated to his eye doctor.

The condition slowed Ted's work in the middle part of the decade, and he concentrated less on his "big books," instead spending more time on the shorter Beginner Books. He also continued with his increased public appearances, including the acceptance of an honorary degree from his alma mater Dartmouth in 1977. There Ted delivered one of the shortest commencement addresses on record—a verse one minute and 15 seconds long. Titled "My Uncle Terwilliger on the Art of Eating Popovers," Ted advised the graduating class, "as *you* partake of the world's bill of fare/ that's darned good advice to follow. Do a lot of spitting out the hot air/ And be careful what you swallow."

The seemingly antiestablishment advice was welcomed from Dr. Seuss, now 73 years old, and Ted used its success to speak in verse at other public functions. But as Ted neared his 75th birthday on March 2, 1979, much of the media used the occasion as a reason to write about Ted, and he quickly grew tired of talking about how old he was getting. "I meet old, old people, who can scarcely walk, and they say, 'I was brought up on your books,'" Ted told one reporter.

But during this period he also offered some insight as to his creative process. In one interview, Ted said that his basic motivation to write was a license to exaggerate. "I really enjoy overstating for the purpose of getting a laugh," he said. "It's very flattering, that laugh, and at the same time it gives pleasure to the audience and accomplishes more than writing very serious things."

The Butter Battle and Other Fights

But Ted did write about very serious things. As far back as *Horton Hears a Who!*, Ted was concerned with social issues such as equality. *The Lorax* had been his most blatant social statement, but as the 1970s drew to a close Ted was about to take his social conscience a step further.

In 1981 Ted began work on a book titled *Hunches in Bunches*. It was the first "big book" he had undertaken in nearly a decade, but his work was soon cut short when he suffered a minor heart attack. He recuperated to finish the book, which was published in 1982. But more health problems awaited the aging author. A cancerous tumor was discovered in Ted's mouth, and weeks of treatment followed. Upon his recovery, Ted began work on his new social concern: nuclear proliferation.

Always a hard worker, Ted threw himself into his new project with abandon. In letters, he called *The Butter Battle Book* his best book and sought consultation from military friends about its theme in which two tribes, the Yooks and the Zooks, begin an escalation of weapons as they head toward a mutually assured destruction of each other. The story was a direct parable of the nuclear arms race that had begun 30 years earlier between the United States and the Soviet Union.

Soon he was working between eight and ten hours a day on *The Butter Battle Book*, and it was being talked about as "the most important book Dr. Seuss has ever created." But not everyone was enamored with Ted's new title. When *The Butter Battle Book* appeared on Ted's 80th birthday on March 2, 1984, some critics said the book's message was too frightening for young children. But the book was soon selling like crazy and climbing the best-seller lists.

Its publication was something of a triumph for Ted, who had had to take several months off from writing after a cancerous tumor was discovered in his neck. Following a surgery in December 1983, he spent most of the winter on the mend. But the success of *The Butter Battle Book* was only one of the joys Ted experienced during that period. In April 1984 a reporter called Ted to ask him how he felt about winning the Pulitzer Prize for his contribution to education and children's literature.

Ted, who had spent so many years avoiding cameras and television appearances whenever possible, was suddenly everywhere. He even began granting interviews on TV and seemed to take all the recognition in stride. "When you get to be 80," he told one reporter, "people will recognize you on the streets too."

7

YOU'RE ONLY OLD ONCE

As Ted advanced into his 80s, there was no denying the toll age was taking on him. But even when he had been at his most ill, Ted had never enjoyed visits to the doctor. Recommendations as to how he could improve his health were ignored if Ted did not agree with them—which was often. So, in typical Seussian fashion, he turned his ailments into the subject of a book: *You're Only Old Once!*

The story is about an unnamed man who checks into a clinic for "spleen readjustment and muffler repair," where he undergoes a series of tests and is told, "You're in pretty good shape/ For the shape you're in." The book discussed the hardships of getting older and the difficulties of being put at the mercy of doctors and hospitals. Ted admitted that it was his most autobiographical book yet.

You're Only Old Once! was Ted's 45th book. Published on his 82nd birthday, the book was an immediate hit, although some readers felt it appealed more to adults than children. In fact, the book was subtitled: "A Book for Obsolete Children," which Ted believed described at least a quarter of his readers. Most had grown up with Ted, and now they were reading his books to their children.

The book quickly jumped to the top of best-seller lists, and within a year it had sold more than a million copies. But for Ted its success was more than simply sales. It was clear now that Ted wasn't writing only for school-age children; he was writing for kids "ages 95 and down."

Seuss in Retrospect

As Ted's health continued to deteriorate through the 1980s, he made fewer and fewer public appearances. A career retrospective opened in 1986 at the San Diego Museum of Art, which helped to cement Ted's reputation as an artist. That had been one of Ted's concerns for years. He was worried that people perceived him as an illustrator or an author of children's books, not as an actual artist.

The exhibition traveled to museums around the country, and Ted was granted a special tribute in his hometown of Springfield. But it was clear to those around him that Ted's career was nearing its end. Ted was spending more time at the Tower, and in 1987 two milestones passed: Ted's first book, *And to Think That I Saw It on Mulberry Street*, had its 50th anniversary, and *The Cat in the Hat* turned 30 years old.

Ted completed the text for his final Beginner Book, *I Am Not Going to Get Up Today!*, the same year, and the illustrations were drawn by an artist named James Stevenson. It was his first title for the series in eight years. But Ted was also at work on another project that had come together quite by accident. He was still spending nearly eight hours a day working in his studio, and a series of pen-and-ink drawings began to materialize into *Oh, the Places You'll Go!*, Ted's final book.

The story was a tribute to the many adventures life holds and a call to action. It urged readers to get on with their lives. But while the book talked about all the great things that could happen to a person, it also advised that there will be times of difficulty: "So be sure when you step./ Step with care and great tact/ and remember that Life's/ a Great Balancing Act."

When the book was published in 1990, it was an immediate hit, shooting to the top of *The New York Times*'s adult best-seller list. That news made Ted ecstatic. "I no longer write for children. I write for *people*!" he said.

On to a New Place

Oh, the Places You'll Go! became a literary blockbuster. Even by Dr. Seuss standards, the book would break sales records and go on to become Ted's best-selling title. However, by this time Ted's life had slowed remarkably. He spent most days at home, as he organized his affairs and prepared for the inevitable. The following year, on September 24, 1991, Theodor Seuss Geisel died in his sleep. He was 87 years old.

Ted's death was a somber occasion for much of the country. Newspaper cartoonists and columnists, television commentators, and even politicians eulogized Ted. At Dartmouth, his alma mater, a 24-hour vigil was held as students read aloud from his books, and even the comedy show *Saturday Night Live* paid special tribute with a reading of *Green Eggs and Ham*. The world had lost a one-of-a-kind talent.

But Ted's passing did little to dampen the enthusiasm for his books. *Oh, the Places You'll Go!* continued to be a best-seller, and Random House put out a number of posthumous releases that Ted had worked on before his death, including the popular *Daisy-head Mayzie*, in 1994.

Audrey Geisel created Dr. Seuss Enterprises, an organization dedicated to protecting Ted's name and copyrights. Few projects associated with Dr. Seuss were allowed to move forward, and it took producers years to convince Audrey to allow them to make a film based on *How the Grinch Stole Christmas!* The movie, starring Jim Carrey, was finally OK'd and hit theaters in 2000. A film based on *The Cat in the Hat* followed a couple years later. A Broadway show titled *Seussical* debuted in 2000, and 2004—the 100th anniversary of Ted's birth—provided a new and welcome occasion on which to honor Ted.

In addition to receiving a star on Hollywood's Walk of Fame, Ted was honored by the United States Postal Service in a commemorative stamp. In 2005 the American Library Association created the Theodor Seuss Geisel Award, which will be handed out annually to an author and illustrator of an outstanding book for beginning readers.

In his life and work, Ted respected children as individuals with great potential. (Photofest)

Toward the end of his life, Ted sat down to an interview in which many of the same questions he had heard before were asked. One topic that had come up repeatedly struck a chord with Ted, and he said to the interviewer, "I keep getting asked the question, 'Do you like children?' I like children in the same way that I like people. There are some stinkers among children as well as among adults. I like or dislike them as individuals." It was the same sort of fairness that he had displayed in all his books. There was no favoritism; no one was better than anyone else—children included.

TIME LINE

1904 Born March 2 in Springfield, Massachusetts

1921 Leaves home for Dartmouth

1924 Elected editor in chief for Dartmouth newspaper *Jack-O-Lantern*; first uses "Seuss" pseudonym

1925 Graduates from Dartmouth, goes to Oxford

1926 Leaves school to work as a freelance cartoonist

1927 Marries Helen Palmer, November 29

1928 Hired by Standard Oil to draw company's magazine ads

1931 Launches book career by illustrating his first title

1932 Writes children's ABC book but can't find a publisher

1937 First children's book, *And to Think That I Saw It on Mulberry Street*, is published under the name Dr. Seuss

1938 Second book, *The 500 Hats of Bartholomew Cubbins*, is published

1939 Writes *The Seven Lady Godivas* and *The King's Stilts*

1940 *Horton Hatches the Egg* is published and, with its playful language and unique illustrations, becomes the title by which future Seuss books are defined

1942 Starts publishing political cartoons for the New York daily *PM*

1943 Inducted into Army at age 38, where he makes documentary films

1947 *McElligot's Pool* published, first book in seven years

1948 *Thidwick, the Big-Hearted Moose* published

1950 Introduces fantasy characters such as the Joats, Chuggs and Natches in *If I Ran the Zoo*; fantastic characters become a Seuss staple

1954 Helen falls ill; John Hersey article complains about young readers' books, which inspires Ted

1955 Receives honorary doctorate from Dartmouth; Helen recovers

1957 *The Cat in the Hat* is published; Beginner Books formed; *How the Grinch Stole Christmas!* published

1960 Writes *Green Eggs and Ham*, using only 50 words

1967 Helen dies on October 23

1968 Marries Audrey Stone Dimond; Bright & Early Books series launched

1971 Writes *The Lorax*, which criticizes wasteful behavior

1977 Receives honorary degree from Dartmouth

1984 Publishes *The Butter Battle Book*, a parable of the nuclear arms race; wins Pulitzer Prize for contributions to children's education and literature

1986 *You're Only Old Once!*, Ted's "Book for Obsolete Children" is published

1990 Most successful book is published: *Oh, the Places You'll Go!*

1991 Dies September 24, in La Jolla, California

HOW TO BECOME AN ILLUSTRATOR

THE JOB

Illustrators create artwork for both commercial and fine art purposes. They use a variety of media—pencil, pen and ink, pastels, paints (oil, acrylic, and watercolor), airbrush, collage, and computer technology. Illustrations are used to decorate, describe, inform, clarify, instruct, and draw attention. They appear everywhere in print and electronic formats, including books, magazines, newspapers, signs and billboards, packaging (for everything from milk cartons to CDs), websites, computer programs, greeting cards, calendars, stationery, and direct mail.

Illustrators often work as part of a creative team, which can include graphic designers, photographers, and individuals who draw lettering called *calligraphers.* Illustrators work in almost every industry. Medical illustration and fashion illustration are two of the fastest growing specialties.

Medical illustrators use graphics, drawings, and photographs to make medical concepts and descriptions easier to understand. Medical illustrators provide illustrations of anatomical and biological structures and processes, as well as surgical and medical techniques and procedures. Their work is found in medical textbooks, magazines and journals, advertisements for medical products, instructional films and videotapes, television programs, exhibits, lectures and presentations, and computer-assisted learning programs. Some medical illustrators create three-dimensional physical models, such as anatomical teaching models, models used for teaching medical procedures, and also prosthetics.

Medical illustrators generally work with physicians, surgeons, biologists, and other scientists. When detailing a surgical procedure, they may observe the surgeon during surgery, and take instruction and advice from the surgeon about which parts of an operation to illustrate. They may illustrate parts of the body: the eye, the skeletal structure, the muscular structure, the structure of a cell, etc., for textbooks, encyclopedias, medical product brochures, and related literature. They may work with researchers to identify new organisms, develop new drugs, and examine cell structures, illustrating aspects of the researchers' work. They may also assist in developing sophisticated computer simulations, which allow physicians in training to "perform" a surgical procedure entirely on a computer before they are skilled enough to operate on actual patients. Medical illustrators also animate physical, biological, and anatomical processes for films and videotapes.

A medical illustrator may work in a wide range of medical and biological areas or specialize in a particular area, such as cell structure, blood, disease, or the eye. Much of their work is done with computers; however, they must still have strong skills in traditional drawing and drafting techniques.

Fashion illustrators work in a glamorized, intense environment. Their artistic focus is specifically on styles of clothing and personal image. Illustrators can work in a few different categories of the fashion field. They provide artwork to accompany editorial pieces in magazines such as *Glamour*, *Redbook*, and *Vogue* and newspapers such as *Women's Wear Daily*. Catalog companies employ fashion illustrators to provide the artwork that sells their merchandise.

Fashion illustrators also work with fashion designers, editors, and models. They make sketches from designers' notes or they may sketch live models during runway shows or other fashion presentations. They may use pencils, pen and ink, charcoal, paint, or a combination of media. Fashion illustrators may work as freelancers, handling all the business aspects that go along with being self-employed.

Natural science illustrators create illustrations of plants and wildlife. They often work at museums such as the Smithsonian Institution.

REQUIREMENTS

High School

Creative talent is more important in this field than education. However, there are academic programs in illustration at most colleges and universities. If you are considering going on to a formal program, be sure to take plenty of art classes while in high school. Elective classes in illustration, ceramics, painting, or photography are common courses offered at many high schools.

Postsecondary Training

To find a salaried position as a general illustrator, you should have at least a high school diploma and preferably an associate or bachelor's degree in commercial art or fine art. Whether you are looking for full-time employment or freelance assignments, you will need an organized collection of samples of your best work, which is called a portfolio. Employers are especially interested in work that has been published or printed. An advantage to pursuing education beyond high school is that it gives you an opportunity to build your portfolio.

Medical illustrators are required to earn a bachelor's degree in either biology or art and then complete an advanced degree program in medical illustration. These programs usually include training in traditional illustration and design techniques, computer illustration, two-dimensional and three-dimensional animation, prosthetics, medical computer graphics, instructional design and technology, photography, motion media production, and pharmaceutical advertising. Course work will also include pharmacology, basic sciences including anatomy and physiology, pathology, histology, embryology, neuroanatomy, and surgical observation and/or participation.

Fashion illustrators should study clothing construction, fashion design, and cosmetology in addition to taking art courses. They should also keep up with the latest fashion and illustration trends by reading fashion magazines.

Certification or Licensing

Illustrators need to continue their education and training while pursuing their careers. Licensing and certification are not required in this field. However, illustrators must keep up with the latest innovations in design techniques, computer software, and presentation technology, as well as technological advances in the fields for which they provide illustrations.

Most medical illustrators are members of the Association of Medical Illustrators (AMI). The AMI helps to establish accreditation and curriculum standards, offers certification in medical illustration, and provides other educational and support services to members and prospective members of this profession.

Other Requirements

Illustrators must be creative, and, of course, demonstrate artistic talent and skill. They also need to be flexible. Because their art is often commercial in nature, illustrators must be willing to accommodate their employers' desires if they are to build a broad clientele and earn a decent living. They must be able to take suggestions and rejections gracefully.

EXPLORING

You can explore an interest in this career by taking art courses. Artists can always improve their drawing skills by practicing on their own, either producing original artwork, or making sketches from drawings that appear in textbooks and reference manuals that relate to their interests. Participation in art, science, and fashion clubs is also good exposure.

EMPLOYERS

More than half of all visual artists are self-employed. Illustrators who are not self-employed work in advertising agencies, design firms, commercial art and reproduction firms, or printing and publishing firms. They are also employed in the motion picture and television industries, wholesale and retail trade establishments, and public relations firms.

Medical illustrators are employed at hospitals, medical centers, schools, laboratories, pharmaceutical companies, medical and scientific publishers, and advertising agencies. Fashion illustrators are employed at magazines, newspapers, and catalog companies.

STARTING OUT

Graduates of illustration programs should develop a portfolio of their work to show to prospective employers or clients. Most schools offer career counseling and job placement assistance to their graduates. Job ads and employment agencies are also potential sources for locating work.

Medical illustrators can also find job placement assistance with the AMI. In addition to the job leads, AMI also provides certification that is often preferred by employers.

ADVANCEMENT

After an illustrator gains experience, he or she will be given more challenging and unusual work. Those with strong computer skills will have the best chances for advancement. Illustrators can advance by developing skills in a specialized area, or even starting their own business. Illustrators can also go into teaching, in colleges and universities at the undergraduate and graduate levels.

EARNINGS

The pay for illustrations can be as little as a byline, though in the beginning of your career it may be worth it just to get exposure. Some illustrators can earn several thousand dollars for a single illustration. Freelance work is often uncertain because of the fluctuation in pay rates and steadiness of work. The U.S. Department of Labor reports that median earnings for salaried fine artists, including painters, sculptors, and illustrators, were $35,260 a year in 2002. The top 10 percent earned more than $73,560 and the bottom 10 percent earned less than $16,900.

Illustrators generally receive good benefits, including health and life insurance, pension plans, and vacation, sick, and holiday pay.

WORK ENVIRONMENT

Illustrators generally work in clean, well-lit offices. They spend a great deal of time at their desks, whether in front of a computer or at the drafting table. Medical illustrators are sometimes required to visit operating rooms and other health care settings. Fashion illustrators may be required to attend fashion shows and other industry events. Because the fashion world is extremely competitive and fast-paced, fashion illustrators tend to work long hours under the pressure of deadlines and demanding personalities.

OUTLOOK

Employment of visual artists is expected to grow about as fast as the average for all occupations through 2012, according to the *Occupational Outlook Handbook.* The growth of the Internet should provide opportunities for illustrators, although the increased use of computer-aided design systems is a threat because individuals do not necessarily need artistic talent or training to use them.

The employment outlook for medical illustrators is very good. Because there are only a few graduate programs in medical illustration with small graduation classes, medical illustrators will find great demand for their skills. The field of medicine and science in general is always growing, and medical illustrators will be needed to depict new techniques, procedures, and discoveries.

The outlook for careers in fashion illustration is dependent on the businesses of magazine publishing and advertising. Growth of advertising and public relations agencies will provide new jobs. The popularity of American fashion in other parts of the world will also create a demand for fashion illustrators to provide the artwork needed to sell to a global market.

TO LEARN MORE ABOUT ILLUSTRATORS

BOOKS

All about Techniques in Illustration. Hauppauge, N.Y.: Barron's Educational, 2001.

Fleishman, Michael. *Starting Your Career as a Freelance Illustrator or Graphic Designer.* New York: Watson-Guptill, 2001.

Heller, Stephen. *The Education of an Illustrator.* New York: Allworth Press, 2000.

Howard, Rob. *The Illustrator's Bible.* New York: Watson-Guptill, 1993.

Shulevitz, Uri. *Writing with Pictures: How to Write and Illustrate Children's Books.* New York: Watson-Guptill, 1997.

ORGANIZATIONS AND WEBSITES

This organization is committed to improving conditions for all creators of graphic art and to raising standards for the entire industry. For information, contact

Graphic Artists Guild
90 John Street, Suite 403
New York, NY 10038-3202
Tel: 212-791-3400
http://www.gag.org

For information on membership, contact

Society of Children's Book Writers and Illustrators
8271 Beverly Boulevard
Los Angeles, CA 90048
Tel: 323-782-1010
Email: scbwi@scbwi.org
http://www.scbwi.org

This national institution promotes and stimulates interest in the art of illustration by offering exhibits, lectures, educational programs, and social exchange. For information, contact

Society of Illustrators
128 East 63rd Street
New York, NY 10021-7303
Tel: 212-838-2560
Email: si1901@aol.com
http://www.societyillustrators.org

HOW TO BECOME A WRITER

THE JOB

Writers work in the field of communications. Specifically, they deal with the written word, whether it is destined for the printed page, broadcast, computer screen, or live theater. The nature of their work is as varied as the materials they produce: books, magazines, trade journals, newspapers, technical reports, company newsletters and other publications, advertisements, speeches, scripts for motion picture and stage productions, and scripts for radio and television broadcast. Writers develop ideas and write for all media.

Prose writers for newspapers, magazines, and books share many of the same duties. First they come up with an idea for an article or book from their own interests or are assigned a topic by an editor. The topic is of relevance to the particular publication. (For example, a writer for a magazine on parenting may be assigned an article on car seat safety.) Then writers begin gathering as much information as possible about the subject through library research, interviews, the Internet, observation, and other methods. They keep extensive notes from which they draw material for their project. Once the material has been organized and arranged in logical sequence, writers prepare a written outline. The process of developing a piece of writing is exciting, although it can also involve detailed and solitary work. After researching an idea, a writer might discover that a different perspective or related topic would be more effective, entertaining, or marketable.

When working on assignment, writers submit their outlines to an editor or other company representative for approval. Then they write a first draft of the manuscript, trying to put the material into words that will have the desired effect on their audience. They often rewrite or polish sections of the material as they proceed, always searching for just the right way of imparting information or expressing an idea or opinion. A manuscript may be reviewed, corrected, and revised numerous times before a final copy is submitted. Even after that, an editor may request additional changes.

Writers for newspapers, magazines, or books often specialize in their subject matter. Some writers might have an educational background that allows them to give critical interpretations or analyses. For example, a health or science writer for a newspaper typically has a degree in biology and can interpret new ideas in the field for the average reader.

Columnists or commentators analyze news and social issues. They write about events from the standpoint of their own experience or opinion. *Critics* review literary, musical, or artistic works and performances. *Editorial writers* write on topics of public interest, and their comments, consistent with the viewpoints and policies of their employers, are intended to stimulate or mold public opinion. Newswriters work for newspapers, radio, or TV news departments, writing news stories from notes supplied by reporters or wire services.

Corporate writers and writers for nonprofit organizations have a wide variety of responsibilities. These writers may work in such places as a large insurance corporation or for a small nonprofit religious group, where they may be required to write news releases, annual reports, speeches for the company head, or public relations materials. Typically they are assigned a topic with length requirements for a given project. They may receive raw research materials, such as statistics, and they are expected to conduct additional research, including personal interviews. These writers must be able to write quickly and accurately on short deadlines, while also working with people whose primary job is not in the communications field. The written work is submitted to a supervisor and often a legal department for approval; rewrites are a normal part of this job.

Copywriters write copy that is primarily designed to sell goods and services. Their work appears as advertisements in newspapers, magazines, and other publications or as commercials on radio and television broadcasts. Sales and marketing representatives first provide information on the product and help determine the style and length of the copy. The copywriters conduct additional research and interviews; to formulate an effective approach, they study advertising trends and review surveys of consumer preferences. Armed with this information, copywriters write a draft that is submitted to the account executive and the client for approval. The copy is often returned for correction and revision until everyone involved is satisfied. Copywriters, like corporate writers, may also write articles, bulletins, news releases, sales letters, speeches, and other related informative and promotional material. Many copywriters are employed in advertising agencies. They also may work for public relations firms or in communications departments of large companies.

Technical writers can be divided into two main groups: those who convert technical information into material for the general public, and those who convey technical information between professionals. Technical writers in the first group may prepare service manuals or handbooks, instruction or repair booklets, or sales literature or brochures; those in the second group may write grant proposals, research reports, contract specifications, or research abstracts.

Screenwriters prepare scripts for motion pictures or television. They select or are assigned a subject, conduct research, write and submit a plot outline and narrative synopsis (treatment), and confer with the producer and/or director about possible revisions. Screenwriters may adapt books or plays for film and television dramatizations. They often collaborate with other screenwriters and may specialize in a particular type of script or writing.

Playwrights do similar writing for the stage. They write dialogue and describe action for plays that may be tragedies, comedies, or dramas, with themes sometimes adapted from fictional, historical, or narrative sources. Playwrights combine the elements of action, conflict, purpose, and resolution to depict events from real or imaginary life. They often make revisions even while the play is in rehearsal.

Continuity writers prepare the material read by radio and television announcers to introduce or connect various parts of their programs.

Novelists and short story writers create stories that may be published in books, magazines, or literary journals. They take incidents from their own lives, from news events, or from their imaginations and create characters, settings, actions, and resolutions. *Poets* create narrative, dramatic, or lyric poetry for books, magazines, or other publications, as well as for special events such as commemorations. These writers may work with literary agents or editors who help guide them through the writing process, which includes research of the subject matter and an understanding of the intended audience. Many universities and colleges offer graduate degrees in creative writing. In these programs, students work intensively with published writers to learn the art of storytelling.

Writers can be employed either as in-house staff or as freelancers. Pay varies according to experience and the position, but freelancers must provide their own office space and equipment such as computers and fax machines. Freelancers also are responsible for keeping tax records, sending out invoices, negotiating contracts, and providing their own health insurance.

REQUIREMENTS
High School
While in high school, build a broad educational foundation by taking courses in English, literature, foreign languages,

history, general science, social studies, computer science, and typing. The ability to type is almost a requisite for all positions in the communications field, as is familiarity with computers.

Postsecondary Training

Competition for writing jobs almost always demands the background of a college education. Many employers prefer you have a broad liberal arts background or majors in English, literature, history, philosophy, or one of the social sciences. Other employers desire communications or journalism training in college. Occasionally a master's degree in a specialized writing field may be required. A number of schools offer courses in journalism, and some of them offer courses or majors in book publishing, publication management, and newspaper and magazine writing.

In addition to formal course work, most employers look for practical writing experience. If you have served on high school or college newspapers, yearbooks, or literary magazines, or if you have worked for small community newspapers or radio stations, even in an unpaid position, you will be an attractive candidate. Many book publishers, magazines, newspapers, and radio and television stations have summer internship programs that provide valuable training if you want to learn about the publishing and broadcasting businesses. Interns do many simple tasks, such as running errands and answering phones, but some may be asked to perform research, conduct interviews, or even write some minor pieces.

Writers who specialize in technical fields may need degrees, concentrated course work, or experience in specific subject areas. This applies frequently to engineering, business, or one of the sciences. Also, technical communications is a degree now offered at many universities and colleges.

If you wish to enter positions with the federal government, you will have to take a civil service examination and meet certain specified requirements, according to the type and level of position.

Other Requirements

To be a writer, you should be creative and able to express ideas clearly, have a broad general knowledge, be skilled in research techniques, and be computer literate. Other assets include curiosity, persistence, initiative, resourcefulness, and an accurate memory. For some jobs—on a newspaper, for example, where the activity is hectic and deadlines are short—the ability to concentrate and produce under pressure is essential.

EXPLORING

As a high school or college student, you can test your interest and aptitude in the field of writing by serving as a reporter or writer on school newspapers, yearbooks, and literary magazines. Various writing courses and workshops will provide the opportunity to sharpen your writing skills.

Small community newspapers and local radio stations often welcome contributions from outside sources, although they may not have the resources to pay for them. Jobs in bookstores, magazine shops, and even newsstands will offer you a chance to become familiar with various publications.

You can also obtain information on writing as a career by visiting local newspapers, publishers, or radio and television stations and interviewing some of the writers who work there. Career conferences and other guidance programs frequently include speakers on the entire field of communications from local or national organizations.

EMPLOYERS

There are approximately 139,000 writers and authors and 50,000 technical writers currently employed in the United States. Nearly half of salaried writers and editors work in the information sector, which includes newspapers, magazines, book publishers, radio and television broadcasting, software publishers, and Internet businesses. Writers also work for advertising agencies and public relations firms and work on journals and newsletters published by business and nonprofit organizations, such as professional associations, labor unions, and religious organizations. Other employers are government agencies and film production companies.

STARTING OUT

A fair amount of experience is required to gain a high-level position in the field. Most writers start out in entry-level positions. These jobs may be listed with college placement offices, or they may be obtained by applying directly to the employment departments of the individual publishers or broadcasting companies. Graduates who previously served internships with these companies often have the advantage of knowing someone who can give them a personal recommendation. Want ads in newspapers and trade journals are another source for jobs. Because of the competition for positions, however, few vacancies are listed with public or private employment agencies.

Employers in the communications field usually are interested in samples of published writing. These are often assembled in an organized portfolio or scrapbook. Bylined or signed articles are more credible (and, as a result, more useful) than stories whose source is not identified.

Entry-level positions as a junior writer usually involve library research, preparation of rough drafts for part or all of a report, cataloging, and other related writing tasks. These are generally carried on under the supervision of a senior writer.

Some technical writers have entered the field after working in public relations departments or as technicians or research assistants, then transferring to technical writing as openings occur. Many firms now hire writers directly upon application or recommendation of college professors and placement offices.

ADVANCEMENT

Most writers find their first jobs as editorial or production assistants. Advancement may be more rapid in small companies, where beginners learn by doing a little bit of everything and may be given writing tasks immediately. In large firms, duties are usually more compartmentalized. Assistants in entry-level positions are assigned such tasks as research, fact checking, and copyrighting, but it generally takes much longer to advance to full-scale writing duties.

Promotion into more responsible positions may come with the assignment of more important articles and stories to write, or it may be the result of moving to another company. Mobility among employees in this field is common. An assistant in one publishing house may switch to an executive position in another. Or a writer may switch to a related field as a type of advancement.

A technical writer can be promoted to positions of responsibility by moving from such jobs as writer to technical editor to project leader or documentation manager. Opportunities in specialized positions also are possible. Freelance or self-employed writers earn advancement in the form of larger fees as they gain exposure and establish their reputations.

EARNINGS

In 2002, median annual earnings for salaried writers and authors were $42,790 a year, according to the Bureau of Labor Statistics. The lowest 10 percent earned less than $21,320, while the highest 10 percent earned $85,140 or more. In book publishing, some specialties pay better than others. Technical writers earned a median salary of $50,580 in 2002, with entry-level salaries averaging around $41,000 a year.

In addition to their salaries, many writers earn some income from freelance work. Part-time freelancers may earn from $5,000 to $15,000 a year. Freelance earnings vary widely. Full-time established freelance writers may earn up to $75,000 a year.

WORK ENVIRONMENT

Working conditions vary for writers. Although their work-week usually runs 35 to 40 hours, many writers work overtime. A publication that is issued frequently has more deadlines closer together, creating greater pressures to meet them. The work is especially hectic on newspapers and at broadcasting companies, which operate seven days a week. Writers often work nights and weekends to meet deadlines or to cover a late-developing story.

Most writers work independently, but they often must cooperate with artists, photographers, rewriters, and advertising people who may have widely differing ideas of how the materials should be prepared and presented.

Physical surroundings range from comfortable private offices to noisy, crowded newsrooms filled with other workers typing and talking on the telephone. Some writers must confine their research to the library or telephone interviews, but others may travel to other cities or countries or to local sites, such as theaters, ballparks, airports, factories, or other offices.

The work is arduous, but most writers are seldom bored. Some jobs, such as that of the foreign correspondent, require travel. The most difficult element is the continual pressure of deadlines. People who are the most content as writers enjoy and work well with deadline pressure.

OUTLOOK

The employment of writers is expected to increase at an average rate through 2012, according to the U.S.

Department of Labor. Competition for writing jobs has been and will continue to be competitive. The demand for writers by newspapers, periodicals, book publishers, and nonprofit organizations is expected to increase. The growth of online publishing on company websites and other online services will also create a demand for many talented writers; those with computer skills will be at an advantage as a result. Advertising and public relations will also provide job opportunities.

The major book and magazine publishers, broadcasting companies, advertising agencies, public relations firms, and the federal government account for the concentration of writers in large cities such as New York, Chicago, Los Angeles, Boston, Philadelphia, San Francisco, and Washington, D.C. Opportunities with small newspapers, corporations, and professional, religious, business, technical, and trade publications can be found throughout the country.

TO LEARN MORE ABOUT WRITERS

BOOKS

Amoss, Berthe, and Eric Suben. *Writing and Illustrating Children's Books for Publication: Two Perspectives.* Cincinnati: Writer's Digest Books, 2005.

Bolton, Leslie. *The Everything Guide to Writing Children's Books.* Cincinnati: Adams Media, 2002.

Brogan, Kathryn. *2006 Writer's Market.* Cincinnati: Writer's Digest Books, 2005.

Strunk, William Jr., and E. B. White. *Elements of Style.* 4th ed. New York: Longman, 2000.

Zinsser, William. *On Writing Well.* 25th Anniversary ed. New York: HarperCollins, 2001.

ORGANIZATIONS AND WEBSITES

To learn more about the film industry, to read interviews and articles by noted screenwriters, and to find links to many other screenwriting-related sites on the Internet, visit the websites of the WGA.

Writers Guild of America (WGA)

East Chapter

555 West 57th Street, Suite 1230

New York, NY 10019

Tel: 212-767-7800

http://www.wgaeast.org

Writers Guild of America (WGA)

West Chapter

7000 West Third Street

Los Angeles, CA 90048

Tel: 800-548-4532

http://www.wga.org

TO LEARN MORE ABOUT THEODOR SEUSS GEISEL

BOOKS

Cohen, Charles, D. *The Seuss, the Whole Seuss, and Nothing But the Seuss.* New York: Random House, 2004.

Fensch, Thomas, ed. *Of Sneetches and Whos and the Good Dr. Seuss.* Jefferson, N.C.: McFarland & Company, Inc., 1997.

Krull, Kathleen. *The Boy on Fairfield Street: How Ted Geisel Grew Up to Become Dr. Seuss.* New York: Random House, 2004. *

Morgan, Judith, and Neil Morgan. *Dr. Seuss & Mr. Geisel: A Biography.* New York: Random House, 1995.

Minear, Richard H. *Dr. Seuss Goes to War.* New York: The New Press, 1999.

Nel, Philip. *Dr. Seuss: American Icon.* New York: Continuum, 2004.

Seuss, Dr. *And to Think That I Saw It on Mulberry Street.* New York: Random House, 1964. *

——. *The Butter Battle Book.* New York: Random House, 1984. *

——. *The Cat in the Hat.* New York: Random House, 1957. *

——. *The 500 Hats of Bartholomew Cubbins.* New York: Random House, 1965. *

——. *Gerald McBoing Boing.* New York: Random House, 2000. *

——. *Green Eggs and Ham.* New York: Random House, 1960. *

——. *Horton Hatches the Egg.* New York: Random House, 1940. *

——. *Horton Hears a Who!* New York: Random House, 1954. *

——. *How the Grinch Stole Christmas!* New York: Random House, 1957. *

——. *The Lorax.* New York: Random House, 1971. *

——. *Oh, the Places You'll Go!* New York: Random House, 1990.

——. *One Fish, Two Fish, Red Fish, Blue Fish.* New York: Random House, 1960. *

Weidt, Maryann N. *Oh, the Places He Went: A Story about Dr. Seuss—Theodor Seuss Geisel.* Minneapolis: Carolrhoda Books, Inc., 1994. *

*Children's books

MAGAZINES

Bean, Joy. "Celebrating Dr. Seuss," *Publishers Weekly* (February 2, 2004) 23.

Bernstein, Peter W. "Green Eggs and Me," *U.S. News and World Report* vol. 111, no. 15 (October 7, 1991) 18.

——. "Unforgettable Dr. Seuss," *Reader's Digest* vol. 140 (April 1992) 60.

Bunzel, Peter. "Wacky World of Dr. Seuss," *Life* vol. 46 (April 6, 1959) 107.

Cahn, Robert. "The Wonderful World of Dr. Seuss," *Saturday Evening Post* vol. 230 (July 6, 1957) 17.

Fuller, John G. "Trade Winds," *Saturday Review* vol. 40 (December 14, 1957) 7.

Girson, Rochelle. [untitled], *Saturday Review* vol. 40 (May 11, 1957) 52.

Gordon, James Stewart. "Dr. Seuss: Fanciful Sage of Childhood," *Reader's Digest* vol. 100 (April 1972) 141.

Horn, John. "The Grinch's Gatekeeper," *Newsweek* vol. 136 (November 13, 2000) 68.

Jennings, C. Robert. "What Am I Doing Here?" *Saturday Evening Post* vol. 238 (October 23, 1965) 105.

Kahn, E.J. "Children's Friend," *The New Yorker* vol. 36 (December 17, 1960) 47.

Kanfer, Stephan. "The Doctor Beloved by All," *Time* vol. 138 (October 7, 1991) 71.

Lurie, Alison. "The Cabinet of Dr. Seuss," *New York Review of Books* vol. 37 (December 20, 1990) 50.

Maughan, Shannon. "And Now for Something Completely Diffendoofer," *Publishers Weekly* vol. 245, no. 6 (February 9, 1998) 24.

Scott, A.O. "Sense and Nonsense," *New York Times Magazine* (Nov. 26, 2000) 48.

Seuss, Dr. "If at First You Don't Succeed—Quit," *Saturday Evening Post* vol. 237 (November 28, 1964) 6.

——. "Somebody's Got to Win in Kids' Books," *U.S. News and World Report* vol. 100 (April 14, 1986) 69.

WEBSITES

Seussville

http://www.seussville.com

INDEX

Page numbers in *italics* indicate illustrations.

ABOUT THE AUTHOR

Freelance journalist and editor **Todd Peterson** spent several years writing about music and pop culture in northern California before moving to Las Vegas to cover southern Nevada's exciting entertainment scene. Todd moved to New York in 2001 where he continues to write about a variety of topics and edit other writers' work. When he is not writing or editing, Todd is probably devouring a book or hiding out at the movies. He resides in Brooklyn with his wife and his son.